NURSING and LEGAL LIABILITY

A Case Study Approach

by Elizabeth Hogue, Esquire

NATIONAL HEALTH PUBLISHING
A Division of Rynd Communications

Copyright © 1985 by
Rynd Communications

Printed in the United States of America
First Printing
Library of Congress catalog number: 84-63068
ISBN: 0-932500-35-8

Contents

How To Use This Book

1. The cases appearing in this book are actual court decisions. However, they were extensively edited in order to make them easier to read. The editing included deletion of portions of the body of each case, all footnotes, and all citations to cases made within a decision. If the readers wish to read any case in its entirety, they should first check with a public library to see if legal publications are available. Since most public libraries do not have these cases, readers will need to go to a law library to obtain the entire case.

2. A chart entitled, "How to Read a Citation," is provided at the end of this book. This chart may be helpful to readers who wish to review the entire text of a case since the citation indicates where a case is located. It may also be useful for those readers who are curious about what the letters and numbers following the name of a case indicate.

3. A glossary of legal terms is also provided. Its purpose is to assist readers to better understand the legal terminology which inevitably characterizes even the edited versions of court decisions. Readers should refer to this glossary whenever they encounter legal words and phrases they do not understand.

4. Finally, readers should try to remember that it is not essential to understand all of the procedural aspects of these decisions or all of the legal language in order to derive value from them. It is also important to understand that the more court decisions read, the easier it becomes for lawyers and non-lawyers to understand them. In short, practice is essential.

Foreword

Soaring health care costs and increasing consumer awareness are two of the many factors that are changing our health care delivery system. Nurses can be on the cutting edge of this change because we function as consumer advocates of health care. Although nurses have long been involved in patient education and prevention, other groups are only now developing an appreciation for this focus. Unfortunately, nurses are slow to collectively articulate these unique skills we have possessed for years. We have allowed ourselves to be intimidated by those with a medical focus; we often think that our focus is less valuable and important. Now is the time to strengthen our support, help one another, and prepare for the future. In order to do this we must be able to clearly identify our skills, articulate our abilities and unique role, and prepare ourselves educationally. Professional preparation includes an under-standing of legal issues. Only through proper knowledge of our legal responsibilities and potential liabilities can we prepare to be truly accountable for our nursing care.

Historically, physicians were liable for nursing care. As we work for changes in our Nurse Practice Acts, our independent areas of practice will be clearly identified. Nurses alone will be held accountable in these areas. As we attain more autonomy, we will also increase the risk factor in our practice. The author's commentaries help to illustrate this point. We can no longer lobby for more autonomy and then hide behind the physician's coattail when we are faced with a difficult legal question or lawsuit.

In order to experience the full potential of the nursing profession, we must continue appropriate preparation and planning to increase our protection and to minimize risks. These tasks are necessary in order to realize a greater possibility for success and satisfaction in our nursing roles.

Elizabeth Hogue's continued support and encouragement is apparent in the many seminars that she has conducted for nurses. Her commentaries are easy to understand and have a practical nursing application. We are fortunate to have her support, encouragement, and perspective as presented in this publication.

Maryann Burman Thayer, RN, MSN, CPNP

Introduction

The phrase "malpractice crisis" is surely a familiar one to nurses. No other issue has received more attention in recent years than the issue of liability.

Unfortunately, a great deal of the discussion concerning malpractice often amounts to an old-fashioned "spitting contest." Practitioners say that lawyers have caused the "crisis" because they encourage patients to file essentially groundless suits. Lawyers argue that providers contribute to the crisis by inept medical practices and failure to police their own profession. The patient who has suffered physically and mentally as a result of malpractice seems to be lost in the midst of these warring factions.

Part of the reason for the "war" between lawyers and healthcare providers on this issue is a lack of understanding by one side of the requirements of the other. The conflict is based primarily upon ignorance and misinformation. Nurses have many misconceptions about malpractice, and part of their antagonism towards lawyers may be based upon "fear of the unknown." By the same token, few attorneys have any understanding at all of nurses' roles and functions or of the impracticality of many aspects of the law in relation to nursing practice.

The purpose of this book is to provide accurate information to nurses regarding liability in order that they can better protect themselves from claims of malpractice. Suggestions are also offered concerning practical methods of risk management. If the issue of liability appears manageable, nurses may have a greater investment in understanding and complying with the law.

Nurses becoming familiar with court cases involving liability have initially experienced a great deal of fear about their inability to comply with the law. This fear has diminished over time and with greater exposure. It has also decreased as nurses realize that written material on this issue always reflects the ideal with an implicit understanding that, given the many competing pressures of the healthcare setting, it is not always possible to practice the ideal. Nonetheless, there is value in knowing what the ideal is so that the ultimate goal is clear.

Fear is also diminished by the realization that there are some practical tools available which generally help to prevent liability. These include careful documentation and development of positive relationships with patients.

Nurses frequently want to know how much they should document. From the standpoint of liability alone, there is no such thing as too much documentation. Documentation is evidence, and the more evidence available, the greater the likelihood that a potential suit will be "nipped in the bud" or a case won.

Nurses certainly recognize the necessity of documentation when mistakes are not made, but what about when errors are made? Should nurses document mistakes as well as the fine care they render most of the time? The answer is an unequivocal "yes." Practically speaking, however, there are differences in the way the documentation should be handled. The record of good care should appear in the patient's medical record. Reports of errors should be minimized in the patient's medical record. However, a thorough report should be prepared and forwarded directly to the hospital's lawyer, and to no one else. If this procedure is followed, this report is often protected from disclosure by the attorney-client privilege. It must be understood, however, that the purpose of this procedure is not to hide information from anyone but rather to insure that the best possible defense will be prepared.

Undoubtedly, the most effective precaution against liability is the development of healthy relationships with patients. While practitioners may lose sight of this fact, lawyers can attest to the number of clients consulting with them on matters unrelated to malpractice who will also mention possible suits for liability. In the very next breath, however, clients state that they will never sue the practitioners involved because they are convinced that the practitioners really care about them. The importance of positive patient relationships as a means of avoiding liability cannot be over-emphasized.

Nurses have also correctly observed that a number of the court cases involving liability are not very recent. The primary reasons for this fact are that: 1) the legal principles governing liability have been well-established for a number of years; and 2) because courts base their decisions on precedent or previously decided cases consistent with the principles of *stare decisis*, it is essential to turn to older cases in order to find a thorough discussion of well-established principles. Nurses should be assured that, despite the chronological age of some of the cases in this book, the principles are relevant to nursing practice today.

NEGLIGENCE

Negligent action is conduct which is unreasonable under the circumstances. In order to prove negligence, the plaintiff must show that:

1) the defendant had a *duty* to the plaintiff, which

2) was *breached*

3) *causing*

4) damage to the *plaintiff*.

All four of these elements must be proved by the plaintiff in order to show negligence. If the plaintiff fails to prove even one of these elements, the practitioner is not liable. Therefore, these four essential elements are described in the first four chapters of this book.

Duty/Standards of Care

The duty owed by a practitioner to a patient is the following: Practitioners are bound to use such reasonable, ordinary care, skill, and diligence in the performance of their functions as practitioners in good standing in the same geographical area, in the same general type of practice, ordinarily have and exercise in similar cases. This statement contains three standards to be applied to a particular situation to determine whether the practitioner owed a duty to the patient. 1) Did the practitioner exercise the same degree of skill as other practitioners in the same type of case? Practitioners meet this standard if the treatment rendered is the same as that rendered by a "respectable minority" of practitioners in the same type of practice. 2) Has the practitioner rendered care which compares favorably to that rendered by other practitioners in the same geographic area? This test is often called the "locality rule." This rule has been abolished in some jurisdictions; in others it has been extended to include care rendered in similar localities or in other localities accessible to the plaintiff because of modern, more efficient transportation. 3) Did the practitioner exercise the same degree of skill as other practitioners in the same type of practice? This standard means, for example, that a nurse practitioner is required to use the same degree of skill as other nurse practitioners.

ASSISTANT FOUND LIABLE
FOR NEGLIGENT USE OF STRYKER SAW

The first standard is illustrated by *Thompson v. Brent*, 245 So. 2d 751 (La.App. 1971). In this case an assistant was found negligent because she did not use the degree of skill and care required in removing a cast with a Stryker saw. The plaintiff was cut by the saw and was left with a four–inch scar. All of the experts who testified in this case stated that the standard of care for removal of a cast includes a nick or an abrasion, but not a cut of the type received by the plaintiff. In other words, the defendant had a duty to the plaintiff which was breached.

Thompson v. Brent, 245 So.2d 751 (La. App. 1971)
Louisiana Court of Appeals

The plaintiff–appellee, Alma Thompson, filed suit for personal injuries against the defendants, Dr. Walter H. Brent, his medical assistant, Mrs. Sally Doming, and the doctor's liability insurer, St. Paul Fire and Marine Insurance Company. In her petition, she alleges that while under the doctor's treatment, his medical assistant removed a plaster of paris cast from her arm in a negligent manner. As a result of this alleged negligence, her arm was cut and today bears a residual scar approximately four inches in length and one–sixteenth inch in width.

In removing the cast, Mrs. Doming utilized what is known as a Stryker saw. The Stryker saw is an electric–powered hand operated tool which has a small disc–shaped blade at the end. It does not rotate 360° as a normal electric–powered saw but rotates only a few degrees in one direction and rotates back a few degrees in the opposite direction. Both rotating motions are at a high rate of speed and provide the cutting action against a hard surface, in this case the cast. The Stryker saw is designed to cut hard and unyielding surfaces but will not readily cut softer and yielding surfaces such as the skin. Pressure must be exerted in order for the saw blade to penetrate hard plaster. Once through the plaster and if pressure is not lessened, it is possible for the blade to come in contact with the skin and cause injury.

It is admitted by all medical witnesses and by both counsel that a Stryker saw is utilized by the medical profession as it is the accepted instrument for the removal of plaster of paris casts. It is further admitted that the use of the Stryker saw by a medical assistant as opposed to the doctor himself is the accepted medical practice in this area. There was no attempt to show that the medical assistant hired by the doctor was in any way incompetent or lacked the degree of skill necessary in the use of this instrument and the record shows that this medical assistant was certainly qualified in the operation of the Stryker saw.

The first question thus to be resolved is whether or not Mrs. Sally Doming, Dr. Brent's medical assistant, was negligent in her use of the Stryker saw in removing Mrs. Thompson's cast . . .

. . . The jurisprudence is well settled with regard to the duty owed by a treating physician to his patient. As our Supreme Court succinctly stated in *Meyer v. St. Paul–Mercury Indemnity Co.,*

> A physician, surgeon or dentist, according to the jurisprudence of this court and of the Louisiana Courts of Appeal, is not required to exercise the highest degree of skill and care possible. As a general rule, it is his duty to exercise the degree of skill ordinarily employed, under similar circumstances, by the members of his profession in good standing in the same community or locality, and to use reasonable care and diligence, along with his best judgment, in the application of his skill to the case.

Therefore, if Mrs. Doming met the aforementioned standard, she must be considered free from negligence and absolved from all legal liability for Mrs. Thompson's injury.

All expert witnesses who testified agreed that an abrasion or a nick might occur as a result of removing a cast with the Stryker saw. However, they further agreed that such an abrasion or nick normally occurs in only ten percent of the cases in which a cast is removed. In other words, it is the exception rather than the rule for a patient to be so injured. Furthermore, when an abrasion does occur, it is because of the interaction of three factors—the heat and the motion of the saw blade and the pressure exerted by the technician during the cutting process.

Plaintiff complained most vehemently to Mrs. Doming almost from the outset of the removal procedure that her arm was being cut. In each instance, plaintiff was told that it was only the heat of the blade she was feeling and that she was not being injured. Mrs. Doming admits that despite the fact that plaintiff complained, she continued to use the same amount of pressure in handling the saw. This is contrary to the normal procedure as outlined by Dr. Brent, who stated that when the patient complained in such a manner, the technician should first cease the cutting operation, thereby allowing the blade to cool somewhat and, on resuming the cutting process, should use less pressure than before since pressure is a major factor in causing injury.

Furthermore, Mrs. Doming should have realized that she was causing damage to plaintiff before she completed the cutting procedure. It was plaintiff's uncontroverted testimony that before Mrs. Doming completed the cutting operation, there was blood visible on the layer of cotton just under the plaster of paris cast. It is our opinion that the presence of blood together with plaintiff's protestations of pain were sufficient indications to inform Mrs. Doming that plaintiff was being injured. This being the case, Mrs. Doming should have taken steps to prevent plaintiff's further injury. However, she ignored the plaintiff and continued to remove the cast using the same amount of pressure which she should have realized was causing and/or contributing to Mrs. Thompson's injury. The result is that plaintiff received an injury which has left her with a residual scar almost the same length as the cast itself and the width of the saw blade. Accepting the fact that it is possible for a patient to receive a slight abrasion during the course of removing a cast when the technician is exercising due diligence in performing his job, we do not think that a technician is exercising due diligence when the injury inflicted runs the entire length of the cast which was removed. We feel that this is especially true when we consider that the vast majority of persons having such casts removed are not expected to be injured at all during the procedure. We are therefore of the opinion that Mrs. Doming did not follow the recommended procedure which others of the same profession would have followed when the patient complained of injury. Therefore, we find Mrs. Doming was guilty of negligence.

The second question to be resolved is whether or not the injury plaintiff sustained was an abrasion or something of a more serious magnitude. If the injury were greater than an abrasion, it was not such an injury as one might expect to experience if the technician were using the requisite skill in operating the machine. The trial court determined, after hearing the medical testimony and viewing the scar, that "plaintiff's injuries were of a more serious nature than minor abrasions."

All expert witnesses agree that an abrasion is a brush–burn type injury occurring when the top layer of skin, the epidermis, is violated. A superficial abrasion does not generally leave a scar nor does such an injury bleed for a prolonged period of time. Mrs. Doming testified that in the seven years she had been doing such work, she had never seen permanent scarring result from an abrasion sustained during the removal of a cast. Plaintiff's expert witness, Dr. Stumpf, testified that he likewise has never seen a scar result from the removal of a cast with a Stryker saw. Moreover, an abrasion does not normally bleed for more than ten to fifteen minutes after the injury, according to one medical expert, and yet the testimony is uncontroverted that plaintiff's wound was bleeding an hour later. Dr. Brent himself expressed surprise in his testimony that such was the case. We are of the opinion that, all factors considered, especially the residual scar and the length of time the wound bled, the injury plaintiff sustained was something more than an abrasion. This being the case, it was a greater injury than one could expect to receive if the technician were properly using the Stryker saw and is further evidence of Mrs. Doming's negligence . . .

For the foregoing reasons, the judgment of the trial court is affirmed. Costs of this proceeding to be borne by defendants-appellants.

o **Recap of the Case.** The court found that the medical assistant was negligent because she failed to follow proper procedure when the patient complained of pain. The court's decision that the practitioner was negligent was also based upon the injury to the patient. Expert testimony during the trial established that a patient might suffer an abrasion when a case is removed, but a cut four inches in length is evidence of negligence.

NONPHYSICIAN FOUND LIABLE FOR IMPROPER PERFORMANCE OF LABORATORY TEST

A thorough discussion of the second test, the "locality rule," is contained in *Morrison v. MacNamara*, 407 A.2d 555 (D.C. 1979). The locality rule is measured solely by the standard of conduct expected of other practitioners in the same locality or the same community. The rule was originally adopted by the courts out of a sense of obligation to rural providers. The courts felt obligated to protect rural practitioners who, because of inadequate training and experience and the lack of effective means of transportation and communication, could not be expected to exhibit the skill and care of practitioners in urban areas.

The practical effect of this rule upon plaintiffs was probably unexpected and highly undesirable. In order to prove their cases, plaintiffs must present expert testimony to establish the standard of care. Only a practitioner from a rural area can testify regarding the practice in that particular area. However, practitioners, particularly those in small, rural communities, are reluctant to testify against their colleagues. The practical effect of the locality rule, when strictly applied, is that it is almost impossible for plaintiffs to prove their cases.

However, with advances in communication and transportation, the rationale for the locality rule is not as valid. Thus, courts are inclined to abolish the locality rule altogether or to expand it. The court in the *Morrison* case abandoned the rule altogether, and instead applied a national standard of care.

Morrison v. MacNamara, 407 A.2d 555 (D.C. 1979)
District of Columbia Court of Appeals

Appellant went to appellee Oscar B. Hunter Memorial Laboratories, Inc., a nationally certified clinical medical laboratory located in the District of Columbia, for the performance of a urethral smear test. The test was administered by appellee Tom MacNamara, a clinical technician, who at that time had been employed by appellee Hunter Laboratories for approximately seven months. According to the technician, he administered the test by inserting a cotton swab about a quarter-inch into the penis with appellant in a standing position. Following the completion of the first test, appellant complained of feeling faint. The technician instructed appellant to sit down and rest, and to place his head between his legs. The technician did not attempt to examine appellant or seek medical assistance so that the source and extent of appellant's complaints could be ascertained.

Approximately two to three minutes later, the technician asked appellant "if it was okay to go ahead" with a second test, and appellant replied "yes." The technician then proceeded to perform the test a second time, again with the appellant in a standing position. While the test was being administered a second-time, appellant fainted, striking his head on a metal blood pressure stand and on the tile-covered floor. Subsequently, he was taken to George Washington University Hospital where he was admitted as a neurosurgery patient. As a result of this incident, appellant sustained a number of injuries including a permanent loss of his sense of smell and a partial loss of his sense of taste. Appellant brought an action against appellees charging them with professional malpractice in the manner which they conducted the test and for proceeding with test despite the fact that appellant had complained of feeling faint.

At trial, the principal issue in dispute concerned the appropriate standard of care to be applied to appellees. Appellant maintained that since the laboratory was nationally certified and held itself out to the public as such, appellees should be held to a national standard of care. In this connection, appellant presented as an expert witness Dr. George Shargel, a board certified urologist and a member of the American College of Surgeons, who practiced in the state of Michigan. Dr. Shargel stated that although appearing simple, the urethral smear test involved a highly invasive procedure causing severe pain, particularly if there is disease or inflammation present. He testified that the insertion of a swab into the male organ produces a vasal vagal reflex in a patient which causes the blood to rush from the brain to the area being traumatized, thereby causing the patient to feel faint. For this reason, Dr. Shargel explained, the nationally accepted medical standard of care requires the test to be administered with the patient in a prone or sitting position. Moreover, Dr. Shargel testified that with respect to obtaining a good specimen, there was no qualitative difference between administering the test with the patient in a standing or prone position.

Dr. Shargel also testified that to proceed with a second urethral smear test with the patient in a standing position shortly after a patient complained of feeling faint is contrary to nationally accepted standards of care. He stated that it would be improper to rely solely on a patient's word that he feels better minutes after complaining of faintness. The proper procedure, according to Dr. Shargel, would be to use more objective criteria such as pulse or blood pressure to evaluate the patient medically.

Appellees presented several expert witnesses who testified on the applicable professional standard of care—all of whom were from the Washington, D.C. metropolitan area. Dr. Oscar B. Hunter, the principle owner of the appellee laboratory, testified that the laboratory was nationally certified by the College of American Pathologists and that the laboratory holds itself out to the public as such. According to Dr. Hunter, it is not a deviation from accepted medical standards in the Washington, D.C. metropolitan area or anywhere in the country for the urethral smear test to be administered with a male patient in a standing position. He also stated that the decision to proceed with a second test after the plaintiff had complained of feeling faint was simply a matter of judgment.

Dr. Richard E. Palmer, a pathologist with a clinical laboratory in Alexandria, Virginia, also testified as an expert witness for the appellee. Dr. Palmer stated that he was not aware of any national standards for conducting the urethral smear test, but that in the Washington metropolitan area the accepted procedure is that the test is administered with a male patient in a standing position. Moreover, according to Dr. Palmer, it would be a proper exercise of judgment to repeat the test after a patient complained of feeling faint, if the patient subsequently indicated that he felt better. However, Dr. Palmer stated that he would medically evaluate the patient to ascertain whether the patient was capable of undergoing a second test.

Appellees' final expert witness was Dr. William Dolan, a pathologist and director of the pathology laboratory at Arlington Hospital in Virginia. Dr. Dolan stated that he was not aware of any national standards for conducting the urethral smear test, but that for the past thirty years he has always administered the test with the patient in a standing position. Dr. Dolan stated that if confronted with a patient who complained of feeling faint, he would not only inquire how the patient was feeling, but would also medically evaluate the patient to determine if the patient was capable of proceeding with a second test . . .

. . . The locality rule states that the conduct of members of the medical profession is to be measured solely by the standard of conduct expected of other members of the medical profession in the same locality or the same community . . . The rule was designed to protect doctors in rural areas who, because of inadequate training and experience, and the lack of effective means of transportation and communication, could not be expected to exhibit the skill and care of urban doctors . . .

. . . Even a cursory analysis of the policy behind the locality doctrine reveals that whatever relevance it has to the practice of medicine in remote rural communities, it has no relevance to medical practice in the District of Columbia. Clearly the nation's capital is not a community isolated from recent advances in the quality of care and treatment of patients. Rather, it is one of the leading medical centers in quality health care. The medical schools in the nation's capital rate are some of the most outstanding schools in the nation. The hospitals in the District not only possess some of the most recent medical technology, but also attract some of the best medical talent from all over the country. Moreover, medical journals from all over the country are available to health care professionals in the District of Columbia, serving to keep practitioners abreast of developments in other communities. In short, the locality rule was designed to protect medical practitioners in rural communities, not practitioners in leading metropolitan centers such as the District of Columbia.

Moreover, any purported disparity between the skills of practitioners in various urban centers has for the most part been eliminated. Unlike the diversified and often limited training that was available a hundred years ago, medical education has been standardized throughout the nation through a system of national accreditation . . . Moreover, the significant improvements in transportation and communication over the past hundred years cast further doubt on continued vitality of the doctrine.

. . . In sum, the major underpinnings of the locality doctrine no longer obtain . . .

. . . Quite apart from the locality rule's irrelevance to contemporary medical practice, the doctrine is also objectionable because it tends to immunize doctors from communities where medical practice is generally below that which exists in other communities from malpractice liability . . . Rather than encouraging medical practitioners to elevate the quality of care and treatment of patients to that existing in other communities, the doctrine may serve to foster substandard care by testing the conduct of medical professionals in the same community . . .

. . . We are in general agreement with those courts which have adopted a national standard of care. Varying geographical standards of care are no longer valid in view of the uniform standards of proficiency established by national board certification. Moreover, the tremendous resources available in the District for medical professionals keep them abreast of advances in the care and treatment of patients that occur in all parts of the country. More importantly, residents of the District desirous of medical treatment do not rely upon a medical professional's conforming to the standard of care practices in the District or in a similar locality. Rather, they rely upon his training, certification, and proficiency. "Negligence cannot be excused on the ground that others in the same (or similar locality) practice the same kind of negligence." Substandard practice is substandard whether it is followed in the same or in a similar community.

Although we have found no cases which address the issue of the standard of care applicable to a clinical laboratory, the same reasons which justify the application of a national standard of care to physicians and hospitals appear to apply with equal validity to medical laboratories. Medical laboratories are often staffed and operated by doctors who undergo the same rigorous training as other physicians. The opportunities for keeping abreast of medical advances that are available to doctors are equally available to clinical laboratories. Indeed, medical laboratories are often an integral part of a hospital. Moreover, clinical laboratories generally conduct many of the routine tests that would normally be performed by physicians and hospitals. Accordingly, they owe similar duties in their care and treatment of patients.

Thus we hold that at least as to board certified physicians, hospitals, medical laboratories, and other health care providers, the standard of care is to be measured by the national standard.

o Recap of the Case. The court decided that the locality rule does not apply to a nationally certified laboratory and to practitioners in a metropolitan area like Washington, D.C. Consequently, the court adopted the testimony of the plaintiff's expert who testified about the national standards for performance of a urethral smear test as opposed to the testimony of defendants' experts who spoke only of the standard of care for this procedure in Washington, D.C. The plaintiff won the case.

PRACTITIONER RESPONSIBLE FOR FAILURE TO RECOGNIZE IN ADEQUACY OF OWN TREATMENT

The third standard, that of whether or not the practitioner exercised the same degree of skill as other practitioners in the same type of practice, is illustrated by *Sinz v. Owens*, 33 Cal.2d 749, 205 P.2d 3 (1949). As the court indicated in this case, the standard of care for all practitioners includes a duty to refer a patient to a specialist when a practitioner is unable to render proper care.

Sinz v. Owens, 33 Cal.2d 749, 205 P.2d 3 (1949)
Supreme Court of California

. . . As the result of a traffic accident, Sinz sustained a double comminuted fracture of the tibia and fibula of his left leg. The breaks were just below the knee and above the ankle. He was taken to a hospital in Lodi and, at his request, Dr. Owens was called to treat his injuries. The controversy centers around the treatment given by Dr. Owens upon the basis of a series of x-ray photographs and other evidence tending to show the patient's progress.

The first photographs were taken shortly after Sinz reached the hospital. According to Dr. Owens, because they showed good bone alignment, he applied a plaster cast. The photographs taken immediately after the cast was applied disclosed some angulation, but the doctor stated that he was satisfied with the results as shown by them. Photographs taken about twelve days later indicated further angulation and the absence of callus formation. When the cast was taken off three months after the injury, the angulation was approximately twelve degrees and the callus formation still soft.

By the end of another two months, x-ray pictures showed that the angulation had increased to nineteen degrees at the upper fracture and five degrees at the lower one. At the time of the trial, the angulation was thirty degrees at the upper fracture and the same amount as before at the lower break.

To prove malpractice, Sinz called Dr. Allen F. Morrison as an expert. Dr. Morrison testified that the standard of practice in California is to use skeletal traction on a double comminuted fracture. He also declared that, regardless of the choice of treatment made by Dr. Owens when he first saw his patient, the x-ray photographs subsequently taken showed the need for some form of traction, and traction would have been feasible as late as the time when the cast was removed. Other evidence in the record is to the effect that, at the time of the accident, it was the general custom of physicians practicing in Lodi to refer cases requiring skeletal traction to a specialist in Stockton, about twelve miles away . . .

. . . The voir dire examination of Dr. Morrison shows that he was then practicing medicine in the town of Oakdale, about 27 miles south of Stockton. He testified that his practice was a general one and extended to Turlock, Modesto, and Escalon, the farthest of these places being approximately 40 miles south of Stockton. Lodi, where Dr. Owens had his offices, is about 12 miles north of Stockton. Oakdale and Turlock are smaller than Lodi; Modesto is somewhat larger.

The standard of care against which the acts of a physician are to be measured is a matter peculiarly within the knowledge of experts; it presents the basic issue in a malpractice action and can only be proved by their testimony, unless the conduct required by the particular circumstances is within the common knowledge of the layman . . .

. . . The criterion in this regard is not the highest skill medical science knows; "the law exacts of physicians and surgeons in the practice of their profession only that they possess and exercise that reasonable degree of skill, knowledge, and care ordinarily possessed under similar circumstances." The proof of that standard is made by the testimony of a physician qualified to speak as an expert and having in addition "occupational experience—the kind which is obtained casually and incidentally, yet steadily and adequately, in the course of some occupation or livelihood." He must have had basic educational and professional training as a general foundation for his testimony, but it is a practical knowledge of what is usually and customarily done by physicians under circumstances similar to those which confronted the defendant charged with malpractice that is of controlling importance in determining competency of the expert to testify to the degree of care against which the treatment given is to be measured.

The courts have encountered some difficulties in stating a general rule by which to measure the qualifications of a physician to testify on the issue of standard of care. As developed by succeeding decisions, it has not been uniformly phrased either in language or in substance, but originally, and for reasons of practical necessity, it was based upon geographical considerations which stemmed from the variations in facilities in various communities . . .

. . . It has been said that the theory supporting the rule that the expert must be familiar with the degree of care used in the particular locality where the defendant practices "is that a doctor in a small community or village, *not having the same opportunity and resources for keeping abreast of the advances in his profession*, should not be held to the same standard of care and skill as that employed by physicians and surgeons in large cities." In earlier days, when there was little intercommunity travel, the courts required personal experience with the particular community where the plaintiff was treated as the basis of the expert's testimony concerning the degree of care which should have been used. But the law recognizes that: "The duty of a doctor to his patient is measured by conditions as they exist, and not by what they have been in the past or may be in the future. Today, with the rapid methods of transportation and easy means of communication, the horizons have been widened, and the duty of a doctor is not fulfilled merely by utilizing the means at hand in the particular village where he is practicing. So far as medical treatment is concerned, the borders of the locality and community have, in effect, been extended so as to include those centers readily accessible where appropriate treatment may be had which the local physician, because of limited facilities or training, is unable to give."

But Sinz seeks to advance this development beyond permissible bounds. He argues that "[i]t is a matter of both common knowledge and common sense that the standards of medical practice should be, and in fact are, the same in towns and cities within a large geographic area. For example, the San Joaquin Valley, wherein both Lodi and Oakdale are situated. This court may well take judicial notice of the fact. However, the San Joaquin Valley is an area containing two cities of more than 50,000 population and communities ranging from that number to the smallest way stations. This merely emphasizes the fact that geographical generalizations or localizations do not provide a practical basis for measuring "similar circumstances." In any event, the question as to what constitutes similar circumstances is not one solely for judicial notice of an appellate court. It presents an issue which concerns the competency of a person called to testify as a witness, and must be decided upon a consideration of all relevant evidence.

With regard to the standard of care in Lodi, Dr. Sanderson, who was qualified from occupational experience to compare the standard of care in both places as a witness for Dr. Owens, stated: "I would say that (the) standard in Lodi is just as good as (that of) the average doctor in Stockton." Dr. Morrison, testifying for Sinz, was not personally acquainted with conditions in Lodi but he said that although "usually the smaller the community the lower the plane of care," as to treatment of fractures of this particular nature, the same standard of care prevails throughout California . . .

. . . Considering the testimony of Dr. Morrison and other evidence before the court, it cannot be said that there was any abuse of discretion in the determination that, as to the medical treatment of fractures, the conditions in Oakdale, Lodi, and other adjoining areas were sufficiently alike to make him competent to testify with regard to the standard of medical practice ordinarily followed under similar circumstances.

This conclusion is not based exclusively upon geographical proximity, and necessarily there can be no hard and fast rule laid down as a test for experience requisite as a basis for testimony as to custom and practice. But where all of the towns in which a physician practices are tributary to a city, such as Stockton, and there is testimony that the degree of care at the place of treatment is equal to that in the city, the evidence is sufficient to support a finding of similar circumstances. The essential factor is knowledge of similarity of conditions; geographical proximity is only one factor to be considered . . .

. . . The record shows a "very complicated fracture in the leg" and "one of the most difficult fractures that we can treat." Although there was testimony that, in the circumstances, the ordinary standard of care would have been either to apply skeletal traction or to call in a specialist to do so, the evidence must be considered in connection with the undisputed fact that, at the time of the accident and first x-ray photograph, the leg was in reasonably good alignment. But the successive pictures showed progressive increase in angulation and poor callus formation. According to Dr. Morrison, at the time the cast was taken off, traction still could have been applied and the angulation corrected. The failure of Dr. Owens to recognize the inadequacy of his treatment is strong evidence of a breach of the standard of care testified to by Dr. Morrison.

o **Recap of the Case.** The *Sinz* case is an example of a very difficult aspect of the standard of care, i.e., the inadequacy of one's own treatment. It may be helpful for practitioners to realize that they are not required to provide treatment in every situation. Liability could have been avoided in this case if the practitioner had recognized his limitations and called in a specialist.

2

Breach/Violation of the Standards of Care

After plaintiffs establish the standard of care, they must then show that the standard was violated. Plaintiffs usually show that the standard of care was violated by calling other practitioners who practice in the same specialty or areas as the defendant practitioner to testify as expert witnesses. As previously discussed, practitioners willing to testify against their colleagues were extremely difficult to locate.

CLIENT UNABLE TO FORCE MEDICAL EXPERTS TO TESTIFY ON HER BEHALF

In *Agnew v. Parks*, 172 Cal.App.2d 756, 343 P.2d 118 (1959), a county medical society threatened to exclude members who agreed to testify on behalf of a plaintiff in a malpractice case. The County Medical Association also threatened to cancel their insurance. Since an expert witness cannot be forced to testify by legal process, plaintiffs often found it impossible to prove that the standard of care had been breached, particularly when the locality rule described above was strictly applied. With a relaxation of the locality rule, it became easier for the plaintiff to overcome the so-called "conspiracy of silence" among practitioners.

Agnew v. Parks, 172 Cal.App.2d 756, 343 P.2d 118 (1959)
California Court of Appeals

Suit was filed November 15, 1951, as the result of a series of trials which arose out of a malpractice action brought by plaintiff against Dr. Edwin Larson on July 10, 1945, based upon his failure to take x-rays for injuries to her hip sustained by a fall on March 3, 1943 . . .

. . . Very briefly, the pleading charged a conspiracy alleging that plaintiff sought, for a consideration, to get certain doctors to testify as expert medical witnesses on her behalf in a malpractice case, but was unsuccessful due to threats of the Los Angeles County Medical Association to expel them from membership and cause a cancellation of their public liability insurance if they did so; and that defendants submitted Dr. Larson's defense in plaintiff's case to a "malpractice committee" of the Association on which it rendered an opinion declaring him free from negligence, and published it to each member of the Association; and further alleged that defendants conspired to obstruct the orderly prosecution of plaintiff's malpractice action and cause a concerted refusal to deal, by threatening members of the Association to prevent them from testifying, concealing 18 X-rays of her injuries, and causing the Superior Court on July 14, 1946, upon recommendation of the Association, to appoint Dr. Parks as a "distinguished and unprejudiced" witness to examine plaintiff and testify; that such "recommendation" was in accord with a plan to recommend a doctor favorable to Larson, represent him as being impartial and then have him testify for the defendant; and that after Parks was appointed by the court he appeared at the first trial as an alleged disinterested witness for plaintiff, testifying unfavorably to plaintiff's case . . .

Appellant's real complaint stems from her alleged unsuccessful attempt to secure the expert testimony of nine doctors who refused to testify for her in a malpractice action against Dr. Larson because the Los Angeles County Medical Association assertedly threatened to expel them from membership and report them to their insurance carriers to cause cancellation of their insurance policies if they did so. Although a determination of the issues before us depends upon whether, under the facts alleged, defendants have committed a civil wrong, and the ethical considerations so pertinaciously advanced by an appellant have little place in our resolve of a purely legal problem, however, because of the nature and extent of her argument we are impelled to comment briefly on her scathing condemnation of what she asserts to be a common design among respectable medical practitioners to intimidate members of their own profession to prevent them from testifying against each other and rendering services as experts for plaintiffs in malpractice actions regardless of merit, " 'largely due to the pressure exerted by medical societies and public liability insurance companies which issue policies of liability insurance to physicians covering malpractice claims' ". . .

Quite apart from this language and the allegations of plaintiff's complaint, the truth of which we are bound at this point to assume . . . one cannot long be acquainted with our courts without recognizing the existence of just such a serious ethical problem growing out of the surging tide of malpractice litigation which, if not resolved, may well threaten not only the fair administration of justice but irreparable harm to the medical profession which can only result in frustration of public confidence in, and an impugnation of the integrity of, one of the world's most honorable professions. We are acutely aware of the problems arising out of the steadily increasing volume of negligence actions plaguing doctors and that they, more than the members of any other profession because of the serious personal nature of their services, are subject to attack by many unfounded claims of malpractice; but it cannot be denied even by the profession itself that there are also many claims of substantial merit. In recognition thereof our trial courts have encouraged local medical societies to cooperate in the formation of a panel of impartial qualified medical doctors from which they may with confidence appoint experts to examine claimants involved in negligence actions against doctors and give their unbiased opinion, which endeavor has recently been adopted by our State Legislature authorizing the new so-called Impartial Medical Testimony Plan. Perhaps the medical profession, having previously tried to cope with the problem of malpractice litigation in a variety of ways with obviously not too much success, will find that its faithful cooperation will result in the destruction of the ill-reputed "conspiracy of silence". . . said to pervade malpractice litigation, and prevent further serious attacks on the dignity and integrity of this fine profession, and the competent and proficient men and women who comprise it.

Absent a showing in her complaint that any doctor had previously been retained by plaintiff to examine or treat her, we are faced with the question whether a doctor, who has no relationship with a person growing out of contract to examine or treat, has a duty to enter into an agreement to render services as a medical expert merely upon request. We hold that he does not. Even the Hippocratic Oath, by which every doctor is morally bound, assumes a pre–existing relationship of patient and physician, which relationship in its inception is basically contractual and wholly voluntary, created by agreement, express or implied, and which by its terms may be general or limited. . . Since there is no established public policy and no legal obligation compelling him to engage in practice, accept professional appointment, or render medical services to anyone who seeks to engage him . . . we conclude that there is no duty on a doctor's part to agree to serve as an expert witness for one with whom he has no pre–existing contractual relationship. In so holding we do not question the well–established rule that a doctor who has treated or examined a patient may be compelled to testify for him as an ordinary witness and answer pertinent questions concerning facts relating to his condition, knowledge of which he acquired through his examination and treatment even though he discovered them by reason of his special or expert training . . .

. . .Although appellant devotes little time to this point, there arises from her pleading a serious issue of damage. In summary, she alleged that on July 10, 1946, for the purpose of damaging her rights in her malpractice action and knowing such representations to be false, defendants conspired to have Dr. Parks falsely represent to plaintiff and the court that he was a disinterested and unprejudiced witness, would give independent testimony, knew none of the parties to the action, and had not been on the staff of the California Hospital, in order to induce reliance upon them; that she had no knowledge of the falsity of these representations until November 24, 1948, when at the second trial Parks testified he had known Larson prior to the date of the first trial and had served with him on the California Hospital staff; that Parks, intending to give biased and prejudicial testimony for the benefit of Larson, agreed with the Los Angeles County Medical Association to submit himself for appointment by the court as a disinterested witness in the trial of plaintiff's action, and falsely represented to her and the court that he was disinterested, did not know Larson or Pool and had not served on any hospital staff with Larson; that although Parks was well acquainted with Larson and Pool and at one time served on the staff of the California Hospital with Larson, he made contrary representations to mislead plaintiff, which she relied upon believing them to be true; and plaintiff employed Dr. Parks as an "independent and impartial" expert medical witness, paying him $200 therefor and $50 for his examination as ordered by the court, thereby suffering general damages in the sum of $250, specific damages in the sum of $2,500 for court costs and legal expenses in connection with both trials and appeals, and punitive damages in the sum of $50,000. . .

The gist of the alleged conspiracy is fraud . . . Respondents do not seriously contend that appellant failed to properly allege that certain false representations were made by defendants knowing them to be false with the intent to induce plaintiff to rely upon them, and that she relied thereon . . . but they advance the position that the pleading failed to sufficiently allege resulting damage to her. It is the rule that fraud without damage is not actionable . . .

Plaintiff's first item of damage, in the sum of $2,500, is predicated upon her expenditure of court costs and legal fees in the prosecution of two malpractice trials and appeals, none of which were included or legally allowable in cost judgments rendered in her favor by this court on appeal. No further averment concerning this item appears in her complaint—only the general allegation that defendants' acts were done for the purpose of damaging her rights at law against Larson and destroying her effective means of recovery. Therefore, even if properly alleged, the damage plaintiff would have suffered could only have been due to her failure to prevail in her suit and the resulting legal expense to her, the recovery of which would depend upon whether the outcome of the trial would otherwise have been successful; and to show this she must plead and prove a good cause of action for malpractice against Larson, Parks actually gave prejudiced testimony, his fraud caused the trial judge to enter the judgment of nonsuit against her, and had the cause gone to the jury she would have prevailed and in a definite amount. Damage to be subject to a proper award must be such as follows the act complained of as a legal certainty and we conclude that the difficulty in ascertaining damages herein is insurmountable . . .

Although we conclude plaintiff's alleged loss to be too uncertain, remote and speculative to constitute a proper basis for computation of damages, we do not find the item of $250 damage subject to the same objections. She has alleged that in reliance on defendant's knowingly false representations and believing them to be true, she retained Parks as an expert medical witness and paid him $250 for his services, which she would not have paid had she known the truth. So, too, has she properly alleged a general conspiracy, continually referring to the acts of "all defendants" and "each of them," not only in furtherance of a conspiracy, but in creation of a plan to misrepresent Parks to the plaintiff as an unprejudiced witness for the purpose of damaging her. Reading the allegations in the second cause of action as a whole . . . it is obvious they charge concert of action among all defendants according to a definite plan to accomplish the purpose of the conspiracy, their illegal actions in furtherance of a common scheme or design to achieve the unlawful purpose of their combination, and their knowledge of the conspiracy and its unlawful purpose . . . and assuming all of the allegations to be true, plaintiff thereunder would be entitled to compensatory damage in the amount of $250.

Plaintiff's claim to punitive damage is likewise properly pleaded . . . and although she prayed for $50,000, the allowance or disallowance . . . thereof are reposed in the sole discretion of the jury.

Before the first trial in her malpractice case (July 10, 1946) plaintiff communicated with, and personally requested, nine medical doctors, all members of the Los Angeles County Medical Association, to testify for a consideration as expert medical witnesses on her behalf, all of whom refused. Three gave the following reasons: one stated his malpractice insurance would be cancelled and he would jeopardize his membership in the Los Angeles County Medical Association if he testified; another said "the practice of doctors appearing for plaintiffs was frowned upon"; and Dr. Paul McMasters, respondent herein and one of plaintiff's own doctors who would not appear at the first trial but did so at the second, told her "(Y)ou had a pretty rough time, but I could not testify against another doctor," and if she planned to call an expert who is a member of the Los Angeles County Medical Association, he "cannot testify for (you) against another doctor." During a discussion among Larson, Pool, plaintiff and her attorney, the latter stated he was having difficulty getting doctors to testify for plaintiff and Pool, Larson's counsel, said "You will never get a doctor to testify against another doctor. No doctor would dare do it."

Thereafter, plaintiff at the first trial asked the court to appoint . . . a disinterested medical witness to testify as an expert. Agreeing to do so, the judge said "I don't want to appoint a doctor that is personally acquainted with either of the parties or the attorneys. That is a starting point"; he also advised her attorney plaintiff would have to pay to whomever he appointed a fee of $50 for an examination and $100 per day for testifying. The judge then called the Los Angeles County Medical Association and said he was hearing a malpractice case, wished to "appoint a disinterested physician" to testify as an expert in the case, wanted it to furnish the name of a doctor who would be willing to do so, and would like "to get a doctor that was unknown to any of the parties or the attorneys and who would come in and testify as a disinterested witness," giving it the names of the parties and counsel.

Four days later the Los Angeles County Medical Association advised the judge it had communicated with Dr. Floyd Parks; and submitted his name for appointment. The judge asked Dr. Larson and plaintiff if either knew Dr. Parks and each responded in the negative. He then called Dr. Parks and told him he was hearing a malpractice case and wanted "to obtain a physician to testify in the case that was wholly disinterested and unrelated to any of the parties or to the attorneys," and naming each, asked him if he knew any of them. Parks told him he was not acquainted with any of them and was willing to examine plaintiff and testify. The judge then asked Pool and Silver if they knew Parks and each answered "no." He then appointed Dr. Parks and, upon his instructions, plaintiff went to Dr. Parks' office taking her X-rays, where she reminded him he had been appointed by the court to serve as an unprejudiced, disinterested witness and that he did not know any of the parties or their counsel, to which he responded, "I understand that." She asked him specifically if he knew Dr. Edwin Larson and he replied "I don't think so." He then consulted a book wherein two doctors by the name of Larson were listed and after identifying defendant Parks again said in response to her repeated question if he knew Dr. Edwin Larson, "No, I never heard of him." She then asked him had he ever been on the staff of any hospital with Larson, and he said he "had never been on the staff of a hospital with him." Directing his attention to the California Hospital she asked him if he had ever been on its staff and he replied "No, I have never been over there." "Are you sure of that?" plaintiff persisted, and he answered "Yes." Then plaintiff submitted to Dr. Parks her medical records which bore the name of Dr. Edwin Larson on the California Hospital charts and X-rays. Plaintiff believed the hereinabove representations to be true and in reliance thereon engaged the services of Dr. Parks paying him a $250 fee—$150 when he finished the examination and $100 after he testified.

The day following his examination of plaintiff, Dr. Parks testified to the effect that Larson was free from negligence in treating plaintiff. He not only declared Larson had used all the skill and care an ordinary prudent person should have exercised, but voluntarily added plaintiff sustained a second fall which was never mentioned by her and which did not appear in her history, or in his medical report to the court which, on the contrary, stated she had not sustained a second fall.

At the second trial, plaintiff did not request Dr. Parks to testify for her although he appeared and testified as a witness for Larson without compensation and at the latter's request without subpoena.

Parks did not deny that the judge, before appointing him as an expert witness, asked him if he knew Dr. Larson and he responded that he "did not." He admitted that the judge advised him it was his desire to find an expert witness who was not acquainted with either party or counsel and would be "completely disinterested" and unprejudiced. However, he denied he knew Larson until he was confronted with a transcript of the third trial, wherein on cross-examination he was asked "did you, or didn't you ever meet Dr. Edwin Larson at the California Hospital?" to which he answered "I met him there, sure." Then counsel asked Parks if prior to 1946 he ever met Larson in the California Hospital. He said he didn't recall. When asked if when he was Chief Resident there in 1928-29, he ever met Larson, he answered " . . . not that I recall." Shown the transcript of the second trial, he then said, "Well, I think I saw him when I was at the California Hospital . . . I may have seen him, yes." Asked if he became acquainted with Larson he said "Not very deeply, no." He then admitted he had been on the staff of the California Hospital as Chief Resident and it was his responsibility to look over Dr. Larson's records along with those of other doctors and that he saw him at the hospital between July, 1928, and January, 1929; also that when he saw Larson in court at the first trial he connected his face with the name and remembered him, but said nothing about it to the trial judge, the parties or counsel.

The records of the Los Angeles County Medical Association and California Hospital disclose that Dr. Parks and Dr. Larson were admitted to membership in the Los Angeles County Medical Association on the same day, March 4, 1929; that in 1928 Larson was on the Affiliated Staff, on the Associated Staff from 1930 to 1932, and on the Senior Staff of the California Hospital from 1933 to 1953; and that Parks was Chief Resident there in 1928 and 1929, on the Affiliated Staff from 1929 to 1932, 1934 to 1937, and on the Courtesy List in 1938.

Four months prior to the first trial, and on April 20, 1944, the Los Angeles County Medical Association, which has a Medical Defense Committee, published in its official Bulletin an article written by its then President, Dr. Louis J. Regan, a doctor of medicine and attorney admitted to the bar, performing legal services for the Association and advising members threatened with malpractice suits. The Bulletin was circulated among its members and the article related to litigation involving members of the medical profession, specifically to the "alarming and vicious" malpractice trend in California, and the "duty of the medical profession to destroy the malpractice 'racket'." It concluded with " 'The malpractice situation in this community is a miserable one. All our efforts to this time have failed to improve the situation materially . . . It is crystal clear, however, that it is solely and completely our job. Any legal steps to accomplish the desired end should be taken.' "

The evidence also discloses as to insurance, carriers consider nonmembers a poor risk compared with members of the Los Angeles County Medical Association.

It is true that the fact Dr. Parks testified adversely to plaintiff at the first trial does not in and of itself prove that he was prejudiced, but considering this circumstance together with all other proof in the case there appears to be sufficient evidence in the record before us from which the jury reasonably could have inferred that all defendants, together and singly, were unanimous in their efforts to prevent plaintiff from prevailing against Dr. Larson. Whether at the end of the trial plaintiff could have ultimately satisfied the jury of the alleged fraud and conspiracy by a preponderance of the evidence is not at this point material, for this is now no matter of consideration for either the trial or appellate court. In determining whether to grant a nonsuit the trial court is bound to assume the truth of plaintiff's evidence and every inference of fact which may legitimately be drawn therefrom . . .

As to proof of a combination linking all defendants, a conspiracy to defraud may be inferred from indirect and circumstantial evidence . . . from the nature of the acts done, the relationship of the parties, their interest and other circumstances . . . and plaintiff is entitled to a joint recovery of damages against such defendants as she can show have united or cooperated in inflicting a wrong upon her . . . As to respondents Lutheran Hospital Society of Southern California and Adeline Jones, however, we find no substantial evidence in the record that they were part of the alleged conspiracy, knew of, or participated in it . . .

As to respondents Lutheran Hospital Society of Southern California and Adeline Jones, the judgment is affirmed. As to all other respondents, the judgment is affirmed with the exception of that portion relating to the $250 item of damage and punitive damages as alleged in the second cause of action, which portion is reversed with directions that a new trial be had on these issues.

o **Recap of the Case.** Plaintiff needed expert witnesses to testify on her behalf in this malpractice case. She had difficulty arranging the testimony she needed and then attempted to force practitioners who had not treated her to testify. The court decided that nontreating practitioners cannot be forced to testify in malpractice cases; their participation must be voluntary. However, the court also decided that the patient could recover on the basis of fraud and conspiracy because she had been provided with a "disinterested" expert who, as it turned out, knew the defendant.

MENTAL HEALTH PRACTITIONER LIABLE FOR BEATINGS ADMINISTERED TO PATIENT

There are some cases, however, in which the testimony of experts is not required. If the negligence is so obvious that it is within the "common knowledge" of nonpractitioners or "lay persons," expert testimony is not required to show that the standard of care was breached. The classic example of such "common knowledge" is the case of a sponge left inside the plaintiff during surgery. A less obvious example is found in *Hammer v. Rosen*, 7 N.Y.2d 376, 165 N.E.2d 756 (1960). In *Hammer*, plaintiff's claims were based upon beatings administered to the plaintiff by the defendant physician. The defendant claimed that the beatings were part of the psychiatric treatment rendered by him to the plaintiff and demanded that the plaintiff provide expert testimony to prove the contrary. The court rejected the defendant's argument and held that the nature of the acts were proof of a violation of the standard of care.

Hammer v. Rosen, 7 N.Y. 376, 165 N.E.2d 756 (1960)
New York Court of Appeals

Alice Hammer, suffering from schizophrenia, was treated for some seven years by Dr. Rosen, a psychiatrist. In 1955 she and her father instituted this action, the patient seeking damages for malpractice, the father, for breach of contract and for fraud. Their efforts have been signally unsuccessful . . .

With respect to the evidence, it is necessary merely to point out that the testimony given by three of the plaintiff's witnesses, indicating that the defendant had beaten Alice on a number of occasions, made out a prima facie case of malpractice which, if uncontradicted and unexplained and credited by the jury, would require a verdict for the plaintiff.

With respect to the defendant's contentions seeking to justify the dismissal—that the action was barred by the Statute of Limitations, that there was no expert testimony that the acts of assault with which he was charged constituted improper treatment or malpractice and that there was no proof of injury—we may be almost as brief.

Since Alice was insane at the time the cause of action arose . . . the Civil Practice Act effected an extension of the time within which to commence this action. And, since she was still insane when the suit was begun, the defense based on the Statute of Limitations must fail, and it matters not that she had not actually been adjudged incompetent . . . Indeed, even if section 60 had not extended the time to commence the action, the defense would still be unavailing in view of the plaintiff's evidence that the beatings complained of were part and parcel of a continuing course of psychiatric treatment which did not terminate until 1955, the very year in which the action was begun . . .

As to the second of the defendant's arguments—that there was no expert testimony to support the plaintiff's charge of malpractice—the simple answer is that the very nature of the acts complained of bespeaks improper treatment and malpractice and that, if the defendant chooses to justify those acts as proper treatment, he is under the necessity of offering evidence to that effect. In point of fact, the defendant can hardly urge that the plaintiff must call an expert to demonstrate the impropriety of the assaultive acts charged against him in view of the acknowledgement, contained in his brief in this court, that any mode of treatment which involves assaults upon the patient is "fantastic."

And, finally, as to the defendant's claim that there was insufficient proof of injury, we simply call attention to our recent statement that "The damages recoverable in malpractice are for personal injuries, including the pain and suffering which naturally flow from the tortious act" . . . On the evidence presented, a jury would have been warranted in finding that defendant's acts had caused the plaintiff pain and suffering.

The judgment appealed from should be modified by reversing so much thereof as dismissed the malpractice cause of action, a new trial granted as to such cause, with costs to abide the event, and, as so modified, judgment affirmed.

o **Recap of the Case.** The defendant had beaten the patient on a number of occasions. The patient sued, claiming that the defendant was negligent in his treatment of her. The patient did not present any expert testimony during the trial of the case to prove that the beatings amounted to negligent treatment. The defendant then argued that the plaintiff should not win the case because she had not proven that her treatment was negligent. The court refused to accept this argument. The judge stated that no expert testimony was necessary to show that beating a patient amounts to negligence.

3

Causation

After the plaintiff has shown that the defendant had a duty to the plaintiff which the defendant breached, the plaintiff must then show that the action of the defendant caused injury to the plaintiff. The plaintiff must show that the defendant *in fact* caused the injury. The plaintiff must prove that the damage would not have occurred *but for* the defendant's actions. The plaintiff must also demonstrate that the defendant's negligence was a proximate cause of the plaintiff's injury. Proximate cause is usually defined in terms of foreseeability. If the average, reasonable person in the defendant's position could have foreseen the plaintiff's injury as a result of his or her actions, then the plaintiff's injury was foreseeable and the defendant's actions are a proximate cause of plaintiff's injuries.

PLAINTIFF GETS NEW TRIAL IN MALPRACTICE CASE BECAUSE OF INCORRECT INSTRUCTION ON PROXIMATE CAUSE

In *Bender v. Dingwerth*, 425 F.2d 378 (5th Cir. 1970), the plaintiff sued her husband's physician. She claimed that the doctor's negligence caused her husband's death. The facts of this case were that Mr. Bender experienced chest pain during the night. In response to a telephone call, Defendant advised the Benders to go to the hospital. The Benders went to the hospital emergency room. Defendant arrived about one and a half hours later. Defendant's impression was that Bender had early pneumonitis or pulmonary congestion, he prescribed a mild sedative, and admitted Bender to the hospital. Bender died the next morning of an acute myocardial infarction. Mrs. Bender then claimed that Defendant's failure to diagnose heart disease, to consult a heart specialist, to treat her husband like a heart patient, and to perform an electrocardiogram caused Bender's death. She also claimed that Defendant's delay in reaching the hospital caused her husband's death.

After all the evidence was presented, the judge instructed the jury on how to determine whether the plaintiff had shown that the defendant caused her husband's death. The judge told the jury that the plaintiff had to prove that the defendant's actions were the only cause of her husband's death. These instructions were incorrect because the plaintiff must prove that the defendant's actions were *a* cause of injury, not the *only* cause of injury.

Bender v. Dingwerth, 425 F.2d 378 (5th Cir. 1970)
United States Court of Appeals

In this medical malpractice case we wrestle with the usual problems attendant upon such suits and with a particularly difficult one concerning proximate cause, a concept which has all too often thrown judges and lawyers into confusion as though it were a brooding omnipresence in the sky of torts.

. . . Mary P. Bender, the surviving wife of Thomas C. Bender, brought this action on behalf of herself and her minor son against Dr. Frank S. Dingwerth and his partners for alleged acts of medical malpractice occurring in Arlington, Texas. The defendants practiced medicine under the firm name of Arlington Medical Center in that city. The Benders were patients of Dr. Kenneth Adams, one of the clinic partners. Thomas Bender was receiving treatment from Dr. Adams for a diabetic condition which apparently was manageable and not disabling. On the evening of January 21, 1966, Bender awakened about 11:30 p.m., experiencing sharp pain in the chest and difficulty in breathing. Mrs. Bender attempted to contact Dr. Adams, but was informed that Dr. Dingwerth, who apparently had never treated Bender before, was on call that evening. After hearing Mrs. Bender's description of her husband's symptoms, Dr. Dingwerth advised her that he would meet them in the emergency room of Arlington Memorial Hospital twenty minutes later. Dr. Dingwerth arrived approximately an hour and a half later, having waited at his home until the emergency room nurse notified him that the

Benders had arrived at the hospital. After his arrival, Dr. Dingwerth examined Bender and recorded impressions of early pneumonitis or pulmonary congestion. He administered a mild sedative to Bender and admitted him to the hospital as a bed patient, prescribing cough syrup. Bender had a restless night and died suddenly the next morning of an acute myocardial infarction (heart attack).

Mrs. Bender brought this suit against Dingwerth and his partners, alleging several grounds of malpractice: (1) failure to reach a diagnosis of heart disease in view of the patient's medical history and symptoms upon examination; (2) failure to consult a heart specialist; (3) failure to treat the deceased as a heart patient; (4) failure to use the best available diagnostic tool, an electrocardiogram, to reach a diagnosis; and (5) delaying his arrival at the hospital for over an hour.

In its instructions to the jury the court defined proximate cause in the following terms, to which plaintiff does not object:

> By the term 'Proximate Cause', as used in this charge, is meant a moving and efficient cause without which the event in question would not have happened; an act or omission becomes a proximate cause of an event whenever such event is the natural and probable consequence of the act or omission in question, and one that ought to have been foreseen by a person of ordinary care and prudence in the light of attending circumstances. There may be more than one proximate cause of an event.

In another part of the charge, however, the court in instructing the jury on the plaintiff's burden of proof made the following explanation concerning proximate cause, to which the plaintiff does object:

> In a malpractice suit the burden is on the plaintiff to prove by the testimony of a practitioner in the same field of practice as the defendant that the diagnosis or treatment complained of was such as to constitute negligence, and that the negligence was a proximate cause of the patient's injuries; however, the testimony of practitioners in a different field of medicine is competent where the subject of inquiry is common to and equally recognized in all the fields of practice involved. *And the plaintiff's proof in this respect must not only establish the defendant's act or acts as a proximate cause, but must exclude any hypothesis as to the existence of another efficient proximate cause.*

We find the concluding sentence of the instruction fatally deficient. Although the court did not define "efficient proximate cause," we assume that the court meant an act with a causal relationship to the injury sustained. Fairly read, this language instructed the jury that the plaintiff had to prove that Dr. Dingwerth's negligence was, standing alone, the single cause of the death of Thomas Bender and that nothing else contributed to that event. In other words, this charge instructed the jury that the plaintiff in order to recover had to prove that Dr. Dingwerth's negligence was the *sole* proximate cause of Bender's death. This is simply not the law in Texas. In a malpractice case, as in other negligence cases, the plaintiff need prove only that the negligent act of the defendant was a proximate cause of the injury sustained . . .

The plaintiff's burden is thus the affirmative one to establish that the doctor's negligence is one proximate cause of the injury. We have not been cited to nor have we found a single case in which the Texas courts have held that the plaintiff has the negative burden of disproving every other possible contributing cause of the injury . . .

. . . The plaintiff's difficulty in these cases, however, is not a failure to show that the doctor's act was the *only* cause of the injury, but rather the failure to prove that there was any causal act and the ensuing injury. This difficulty usually occurs because the plaintiff's expert medical witnesses are reluctant to state outright that the defendant's act or any other act was a cause of the resulting injury, preferring as medical men to state that such an act *might* have caused the injury . . . The result is that the plaintiff fails to prove what he must prove in any negligence case—that the act complained of was *a* proximate cause of the injury. The rule, therefore, is one demanding strict proof of causation in fact; it does *not* demand that the doctor's negligence be the *sole* or *only* proximate cause in order for the plaintiff to recover. It merely requires proof that the doctor's act is in fact *a* cause.

The charge in the instant case was plainly prejudicial because it imposed on the plaintiff the burden of proving that the doctor's negligence was the sole proximate cause of her husband's death. The defendant, however, asserts that this error is harmless because the judge had in another part of the charge correctly informed the jury that there could be more than one proximate cause and had phrased issue number two so that the jury was properly asked whether the defendant's negligence was *a* proximate cause of the plaintiff's injury. The jury's negative answer to this issue, the defendant contends, precludes liability and renders academic and immaterial any question as to whether or not plaintiff also had to negate other causes in order to establish liability. Indulging as we must in the hopeful hypothesis that the jury parses every phrase of the trial judge's charge, we must disagree with the defendant's assertion that this error was harmless. In the wide spectrum of decisions affecting proximate cause, we have developed a body of dialectics which has given us some boilerplate charges, many of which become logically distorted by the omission, addition or rearrangement of a single word or phrase. Moreover, proximate cause is one of the more elusive concepts developed by our jurisprudence. Its philosophic articulation by a court is difficult enough for a jury to apply empirically under the best of circumstances. When the jury is instead given conflicting instructions, first being told that more than one proximate cause may exist and then being told that the plaintiff must exclude every other efficient proximate cause in order to recover, we think it is impossible to assume that the jury obeyed the former and rejected the latter when it found that the defendant's negligence was not a proximate cause of Bender's death. The distinction between "a proximate cause" and "*sole* proximate cause" is a legal philologist's nightmare. It could hardly be expected that a lay jury would comprehend and correctly apply such a distinction in the face of conflicting and inadequately defined instructions by the court. Because of the court's error in instructing the jury, we must reverse and remand for a new trial . . .

Since this case must be retried because of an error in the court's instructions to the jury, we think it appropriate and in the interest of judicial efficiency to comment briefly on several questions which may arise at the new trial. Plaintiff has here contended that the trial court erred in not allowing the jury to evaluate Dr. Dingwerth's delay in arriving at the hospital by the standard of an ordinarily prudent person rather than by a medical standard. The court charged the jury as follows:

'Ordinary care' with reference to the conduct of the defendant, Dr. Dingwerth, means the degree of care which a general practitioner of ordinary prudence of the same school of medicine and practicing in the Arlington, Texas, community or a similar community would have exercised under the same or similar circumstances at the time and on the occasion in question as determined by the acceptable standards of the medical profession in the Arlington, Texas, community or similar community.

We think this was correct. Though other jurisdictions may prescribe lay standards of conduct to evalute medical negligence, Texas, except in very narrow circumstances, adheres to the professionalization of such standards. The general rule is that negligence in a malpractice case must be proved by the testimony of a doctor of the same school of practice as the defendant doctor . . . The only recognized exception to this rule occurs when the negligence is of a type that is obvious to a layman . . . Therefore, for our court to hold that some lay community standard should apply to the doctor's duty to respond to a patient's symptomatic expositions would be contrary to Texas precedent and, we think, to common sense. Ordinarily a layman should not fashion a doctor's duty because even with our modern diffusion of knowledge some matters are beyond the layman's ken. Under the circumstances of this case, what a competent physician is expected to do is a question for medical experts, not for the butcher, the baker, or the candlestick maker . . .

For the foregoing reason, the judgment of the court below is reversed and the case is remanded for a new trial.

o **Recap of the Case.** The plaintiff claimed that defendant's failure to diagnose heart disease, to consult a heart specialist, to treat her husband like a heart patient, to perform an electrocardiogram, and to attend to him promptly in the hospital emergency room caused his death. At the trial, the judge told the jury that the plaintiff had to show that the defendant's conduct was the only cause of the patient's death. In fact, the law in Texas requires plaintiffs to prove that the defendant's conduct was a cause of the patient's death, not necessarily the only cause. Because the judge's statement to the jury was incorrect, another trial on this case will be held.

PRACTITIONERS, INCLUDING NURSES, LIABLE FOR INJURIES WHILE PATIENT UNCONSCIOUS

Under certain circumstances, however, the plaintiff is not required to prove causation. In some cases the doctrine of *res ipsa loquitur* is applied. In order to apply this doctrine, all of the following conditions must be met: 1) the injury must be of a type which does not ordinarily occur unless someone has been negligent; 2) the defendant must have control of the instrument which apparently caused the injury; and 3) the plaintiff must not have contributed in any way to the accident. In *Ybarra v.*

Spangard, 25 Cal.2d 486, 154 p.2d 687 (1944), the defendants, including nurses, were found negligent based on the doctrine of *res ipsa loquitur* when the plaintiff sustained an injury to his shoulder while under anesthesia during surgery.

Ybarra entered the hospital for an appendectomy. Before he was anesthetized, he had never suffered any injury to his right arm or shoulder. When he regained consciousness, he had a sharp pain halfway between his neck and his right shoulder. The pain worsened and spread to the lower part of his arm. Ybarra developed paralysis and atrophy of the muscles around the shoulder.

Applying the requirements of the doctrine of *res ipsa loquitur* to this case, the court first concluded that Ybarra probably sustained his injuries because someone was negligent. Whatever caused Ybarra's injuries was solely controlled by defendants. Ybarra could not have contributed to his injuries since he was unconscious when they occurred.

Ybarra v. Spangard, 25 Cal.2d 486, 154 p.2d 687 (1944)
Supreme Court of California

. . . On October 28, 1939, plaintiff consulted defendant Dr. Tilley, who diagnosed his ailment as appendicitis, and made arrangements for an appendectomy to be performed by defendant Dr. Spangard at a hospital owned and managed by defendant Dr. Swift. Plaintiff entered the hospital, was given a hypodermic injection, slept, and later was awakened by Drs. Tilley and Spangard and wheeled into the operating room by a nurse whom he believed to be defendant Gilser, an employee of Dr. Swift. Defendant Dr. Reser, the anesthetist, also an employee of Dr. Swift, adjusted plaintiff for the operation, pulling his body to the head of the operating table and, according to plaintiff's testimony, laying him back against two hard objects at the top of his shoulders, about an inch below his neck. Dr. Reser then administered the anesthetic and plaintiff lost consciousness. When he awoke early the following morning he was in the hospital room attended by defendant Thompson, the special nurse, and another nurse who was not made a defendant.

Plaintiff testified that prior to the operation he had never had any pain in, or injury to, his right arm or shoulder, but that when he awakened he felt a sharp pain about halfway between the neck and the point of the right shoulder. He complained to the nurse, and then to Dr. Tilley, who gave him diathermy treatments while he remained in the hospital. The pain did not cease but spread down to the lower part of his arm, and after his release from the hospital the condition grew worse. He was unable to rotate or lift his arm, and developed paralysis and atrophy of the muscles around the shoulder. He received further treatments from Dr. Tilley until March, 1940, and then returned to work, wearing his arm in a splint on the advice of Dr. Spangard.

Plaintiff also consulted Dr. Wilfred Sterling Clark, who had X-ray pictures taken which showed an area of diminished sensation below the shoulder and atrophy and wasting away of the muscles around the shoulder. In the opinion of Dr. Clark, the plaintiff's condition was due to trauma or injury by pressure or strain applied between his right shoulder and neck. . .

Plaintiff was also examined by Dr. Fernando Garduno, who expressed the opinion that plaintiff's injury was a paralysis of traumatic origin, not arising from pathological causes, and not systemic, and that the injury resulted in atrophy, loss of use and restriction of motion of the right arm and shoulder.

The doctrine of *res ipsa loquitur* has three conditions: " 1) the accident must be of a kind which ordinarily does not occur in the absence of someone's negligence; 2) it must be caused by an agency or instrumentality within the exclusive control of the defendant; 3) it must not have been due to any voluntary action or contribution on the part of the plaintiff" . . . It is applied in a wide variety of situations, including cases of medical or dental treatment and hospital care . . .

There is, however, some uncertainty as to the extent to which *res ipsa loquitur* may be invoked in cases of injury from medical treatment. This is in part due to the tendency, in some decisions, to lay undue emphasis on the limitations of the doctrine, and to give too little attention to its basic underlying purpose. The result has been that a simple, understandable rule of circumstantial evidence, with a sound background of common sense and human experience, has occasionally been transformed into a rigid legal formula, which arbitrarily precludes its application in many cases where it is most important that it should be applied. If the doctrine is to continue to serve a useful purpose, we should not forget that "the particular force and justice of the rule, regarded as a presumption throwing upon the party charged the duty of producing evidence, consists in the circumstance that the chief evidence of the true cause, whether culpable or innocent, is practically accessible to him but inaccessible to the injured person" . . .

The present case is of a type which comes within the reason and spirit of the doctrine more fully perhaps than any other. The passenger sitting awake in a railroad car at the time of collision, the pedestrian walking along the street and struck by a falling object or the debris of an explosion, are surely not more entitled to an explanation than the unconscious patient on the operating table. Viewed from this aspect, it is difficult to see how the doctrine can, with any justification, be so restricted in its statement as to become inapplicable to a patient who submits himself to the care and custody of doctors and nurses, is rendered unconscious, and receives some injury from instrumentalities used in his treatment. Without the aid of the doctrine a patient who received permanent injuries of a serious character, obviously the result of someone's negligence, would be entirely unable to recover unless the doctors and nurses in attendance voluntarily chose to disclose the identity of the negligent person and the facts establishing liability . . . If this were the state of the law of negligence, the courts, to avoid gross injustice, would be forced to invoke the principles of absolute liability, irrespective of negligence, in actions by persons suffering injuries during the course of treatment under anesthesia. But we think this juncture has not yet been reached, and that the doctrine *res ipsa loquitur* is properly applicable to the case before us.

The condition that the injury must not have been due to the plaintiff's voluntary action is of course fully satisfied under the evidence produced herein; and the same is true of the condition that the accident must be one which ordinarily does not occur unless someone was negligent. We have here no problem of negligence in treatment, but of distinct injury to a healthy part of the body not the subject of treatment, nor within the area covered by the operation. The decisions in this state make it clear that such circumstances raise the inference of negligence and call upon the defendant to explain the unusual result . . .

The argument of defendants is simply that plaintiff has not shown an injury caused by an instrumentality under a defendant's control, because he has not shown which of the several instrumentalities that he came in contact with while in the hospital caused the injury; and he has not shown that any one defendant or his servants had exclusive control over any particular instrumentality. Defendants assert that some of them were not the employees of other defendants, that some did not stand in any permanent relationship from which liability in tort would follow, and that in view of the nature of the injury, the number of defendants and the different functions performed by each, they could not all be liable for the wrong, if any.

We have no doubt that in a modern hospital a patient is quite likely to come under the care of a number of persons in different types of contractual and other relationships with each other. For example, in the present case it appears that Drs. Smith, Spangard and Tilley were physicians or surgeons commonly placed in the legal category of independent contractors; and Dr. Reser, the anesthetist, and defendant Thompson, the special nurse, were employees of Dr. Swift and not of the other doctors. But we do not believe that either the number or relationships of the defendants alone determines whether the doctrine of *res ipsa loquitur* applies. Every defendant in whose custody the plaintiff was placed for any period was bound to exercise ordinary care to see that no unneccessary harm came to him and each would be liable for failure in this regard. Any defendant who negligently injured him, and any defendant charged with his care who so neglected him as to allow injury to occur, would be liable. The defendant employers would be liable for the neglect of their employees; and the doctor in charge of the operation would be liable for the negligence of those who became his temporary servants for the purpose of assisting in the operation.

In this connection, it should be noted that while the assisting physicians and nurses may be employed by the hospital, or engaged by the patient, they normally become the temporary servants or agents of the surgeon in charge while the operation is in progress, and liability may be imposed upon him for their negligent acts under the doctrine of respondent superior. Thus a surgeon has been held liable for the negligence of an assisting nurse who leaves a sponge or other object inside a patient, and the fact that the duty of seeing that such mistakes do not occur is delegated to others does not absolve the doctor from the responsibility for their negligence. . .

It may appear at the trial that, consistent with the principles outlined above, one or more defendants will be found liable and others absolved, but this should not preclude the application of the rule of *res ipsa loquitur*. The control at one time or another, of one or more of the various agencies or instrumentalities which might have harmed the plaintiff was in the hands of every defendant or of his employees or temporary servants. This, we think, places upon them the burden of initial explanation. Plaintiff was rendered unconscious for the purpose of undergoing surgical treatment by the defendants; it is manifestly unreasonable for them to insist that he identify any one of them as the person who did the alleged negligent act.

The other aspect of the case which defendants so strongly emphasize is that plaintiff has not identified the instrumentality any more than he has the particular guilty defendant. Here, again, there is a misconception which, if carried to the extreme for which defendants contend, would unreasonably limit the application of the *res ipsa loquitur rule.* It should be enough that the plaintiff can show an injury resulting from an external force applied while he lay unconscious in the hospital; this is as clear a case of identification of the instrumentality as the plaintiff may ever be able to make . . .

. . . [T]here can be no justification for the rejection of the doctrine in the instant case. As pointed out above, if we accept the contention of defendants herein, there will rarely be any compensation for patients injured while unconscious. A hospital today conducts a highly integrated system of activities, with many persons contributing their efforts. There may be, i.e., preparation for surgery by nurses and interns who are employees of the hospital; administering of an anesthetic by a doctor who may be an employee of the hospital, an employee of the operating surgeon, or an independent contractor; performance of an operation by a surgeon and assistants who may be his employees, employees of the hospital, or independent contractors; and post surgical care by the surgeon, a hospital physician, and nurses. The number of those in whose care the patient is placed is not a good reason for denying him all reasonable opportunity to recover for negligent harm. It is rather a good reason for re–examination of the statement of legal theories which supposedly compel such a shocking result.

We do not at this time undertake to state the extent to which the reasoning of this case may be applied to other situations in which the doctrine of *res ipsa loquitur* is invoked. We merely hold that where a plaintiff receives unusual injuries while unconscious and in the course of medical treatment, all those defendants who had any control over his body or the instrumentalities which might have caused the injuries may properly be called upon to meet the inference of negligence by giving an explanation of their conduct.

The judgment is reversed.

o Recap of the Case. When the patient went into surgery, there was nothing wrong with his arm. Following surgery, he lacked full use of his arm, and the impairment worsened as time passed. He claimed that the doctors and nurses who operated on him were liable for this injury. The practitioners argued that they were not liable because the patient could not show what or who caused his injury. The court applied the doctrine of *res ipsa loquitur*. Since the plaintiff met all of the requirements of this doctrine, he did not have to show what or who caused his injury to prove negligence.

4

Damages

If the plaintiff establishes the elements of negligence, damages may be awarded to the plaintiff. There are three kinds of damages: 1) *actual*, 2) *nominal*, and 3) *punitive*. Actual damages are awarded to cover medical costs incurred by the plaintiff both past and future, plaintiff's loss of income both past and future, and to compensate the plaintiff for pain and suffering both physical and mental. Nominal damages are awarded when plaintiffs prove their cases but fail to establish actual damages. Punitive damages may be awarded when the plaintiffs show that defendants' conduct was malicious.

PHYSICIAN RESPONSIBLE FOR NURSES' ACTS UNDER "BORROWED SERVANT" RULE

Once negligence is established, damages may be assessed against certain third parties who did not actually perform the negligent acts under theories of vicarious liability. One of these theories is the so-called "borrowed servant" rule. This theory is illustrated by *Minogue v. Rutland Hospital*, 119 Vt. 336, 125 A.2d 796 (1956). In *Minogue*, a physician was found liable for the actions of a nurse in the delivery room who, in carrying out the physician's order, broke several of the patient's ribs. The court reasoned that the nurse was the "borrowed servant" of the physician, and the physician was, therefore, liable for the acts of his servant.

Another theory related to the "borrowed servant" doctrine in *Minogue* is the "captain of the ship" theory. This theory is usually applied to actions taken in the operating room only. According to this theory, the surgeon is held responsible for the actions of all operating room personnel, including nurses, based on the fact that the surgeon has exclusive and complete control over these practitioners, usually borrowed from the hospital for use during surgery.

Minogue v. Rutland Hospital
119 Vt. 336, 125 A.2d 796 (1956)
Supreme Court of Vermont

. . . The evidence as to the material facts is not conflicting. It discloses that the plaintiff, who was pregnant, was admitted to the defendant's hospital, as a patient, on January 20, 1954 at 12:45 a.m. At that time she was in labor and was taken to the labor room in the obstetrical department. There she was attended by two nurses, both of them employed by the defendant and paid by it and one of whom was a registered nurse. Later the plaintiff was taken by these two nurses to the delivery room. She was also accompanied by the doctor who had been selected by the plaintiff to attend her at the time of her delivery and who was not an employee of the defendant and who was present in the labor room at that time.

The plaintiff was delivered of a child at 5:58 a.m. It was a normal delivery. Her doctor was in charge of the delivery with these same two nurses assisting him. During the delivery, the doctor directed the registered nurse to apply pressure. This nurse, in compliance with that direction, applied pressure to both sides of the plaintiff's body on her ribs. The plaintiff testified that the pressure on her left side was so extreme that it felt as though her ribs were being broken and she said, "You are breaking my ribs." The next day the plaintiff complained of pain in the area where the pressure had been applied. An x–ray was taken and it disclosed a fracture of the anterior end of the 9th left rib and also an old fracture of the 8th left rib.

The fee paid by the plaintiff to the defendant for its hospital facilities included the use of the obstetrical department and delivery room and the nurse in attendance there. The plaintiff's doctor, who was in charge of the delivery, had supervision of the nurses while they were in the delivery room.

We are confronted by the facts here with a question that, to our knowledge, has not been passed upon in this jurisdiction.

We, therefore, look to the general principles pertaining to the relationship of master and servant . . . We then will apply them to the facts here presented.

The really essential element in the relationship of master and servant is the right of control . . . The master test is:--Who has the right to control the offending servant in the performance of his work at the time in question? . . .

In determining whether a person is the servant of another, the essential test is whether he is subject to the latter's control or right of control with regard not only to the work to be done but also to the manner of performing it. The true criterion is the existence of power to control the employee at the time of the commission of the negligent act . . .

A servant directed or permitted by his master to perform services for another may become the servant of such other in performing the services: He may become the other's servant as to some acts and not as to others . . . The important question is not whether he remains the servant of the general employer as to matters generally, but as to the specific transaction in question, he is acting in the business of and under the direction of the one or the other . . .

Where a servant has two masters, a general and a special one, the latter, if having the power of direction or control, is the one responsible for the servant's negligence . . .

Nurses, in the discharge of their duties, must obey and diligently execute the orders of the physician or surgeon in charge of the patient, unless, of course, such order is so obviously negligent as to lead any reasonable person to anticipate that substantial injury would result to the patient from the execution of such order on performance of such directions . . .

While the assisting physicians and nurses may be employed by the hospital or engaged by the patient, they normally become the temporary servants or agents of the surgeon in charge while the operation is in progress . . .

Most of the particular cases that we have mentioned involving hospitals, doctors or nurses have to do with occurrences in the operating room. We think the same principles apply to obstetrical cases and to like occurrences in the delivery room. Obstetrics is a branch of medical science which has to do with the care of women during pregnancy and parturition . . . [The statement that] "In the operating room the surgeon must be the master. He cannot tolerate any other voice in the control of his assistants" is equally applicable to the doctor in obstetrical cases in the delivery room.

In the instant case, the doctor was selected by the plaintiff; he was not an employee of the hospital or furnished by it; he had supervision of the nurses in the delivery room and he was the one who directed the nurse to apply pressure. It follows and we hold that at that time such nurse, though a general employee of the defendant, was not its servant in connection with the occurrence here involved. . .

Judgment reversed and judgment for the defendant to recover its costs.

o **Recap of the Case.** This case is an example of the application of the "borrowed servant" rule. The nurse negligently caused injury to the patient by applying pressure to her ribs. Because the nurse was acting under orders from the attending physician who had the right to control her at the time in question, the physician was also held responsible for the nurse's negligent actions.

NURSE LIABLE FOR INJURIES FROM INJECTION INTO OR NEAR SCIATIC NERVE

Under the theory of *respondeat superior*, hospitals may be found liable for the negligent actions of their employees. In *Bernardi v. Community Hospital Association*, 166 Colo. 280, 443 P.2d 708 (1968), a nurse injected tetracycline into the patient's gluteal region. The plaintiff alleged that the nurse injected the antibiotic into or near her sciatic nerve which caused complete "drop foot" and loss of normal use of the patient's right foot. The plaintiff claimed that both the nurse and the hospital were liable for these injuries.

Traditionally, hospitals were liable for the acts of their employees under the doctrine of *respondeat superior* only if the employee's actions were "administrative" instead of "medical." The defendants in this case attempted to avoid responsibility by arguing that an injection is a medical act, not an administrative one, for which the hospital would be liable. But the court rejected this traditional view of *respondeat superior* because there was, in the court's opinion, no reason why hospitals should not be responsible for their actions like everyone else. The court decided that the doctrine of *respondeat superior* applies whenever the person who committed the act producing injury is an employee acting within the scope of his employment. Employees act within the scope of employment when they perform the duties of their employment.

Bernardi v. Community Hospital Association
166 Colo. 280, 443 P.2d 708 (1968)
Supreme Court of Colorado

. . . Lisa, seven years of age, was a patient in the Hospital, having been the subject of surgery for the drainage of an abscessed appendix. The Doctor was her attending physician. He had left a written post–operative order at the Hospital that Lisa was to be given an injection of tetracycline every twelve hours. During the evening of the first day following surgery, the Nurse, employed by the Hospital and acting under the order, injected the dosage of tetracycline in Lisa's gluteal region. It was alleged in the complaint that the Nurse negligently injected the tetracycline into or adjacent to the sciatic nerve, causing Lisa to have a "complete foot–drop" and to lose permanently the normal use of her right foot . . .

. . . The trial court made findings of fact based upon the plaintiff's responses to the Hospital's requests for admissions. These findings include the following: That the Hospital is a nonprofit, charitable corporation; that the Hospital is controlled by a standard of the Colorado State Board of Health to the effect that no medications shall be given except on the written order (or verbal order confirmed in writing) of a qualified, Colorado–licensed physician; that the Doctor was licensed to practice medicine by the Colorado State Board of Medical Examiners and was engaged in the private practice of medicine; that the Nurse was licensed in Colorado to practice professional nursing, i.e., was an R.N., and, under the 1957 Professional Nursing Practices Act . . . and rules adopted thereunder by the Colorado State Board of Nursing, she could administer a doctor–prescribed injection involving the piercing of tissue under and only under the direction of a licensed physician; that Lisa's father, in advance of the surgery, gave written authorization for operative procedure by signing a form which provided in part:

> I certify that the above procedure has been explained to me and I understand the diagnostic or treatment necessary for the operation(s). The Community Hospital, its medical staff, and the employees are hereby released from liability of the results of the procedure.

The Hospital's motion for summary judgment was predicated on the following propositions: That the scope of the license of the Hospital did not contemplate "the practice of medicine" nor the "practice of professional nursing" under Colorado statutes; that the Nurse could act only under the direction of a licensed physician; that under the U.S. Food, Drug and Cosmetic Act . . . the drug tetracycline was limited to "use under the professional supervision of a practitioner licensed by law to administer such drug"; and that the Nurse was "obeying instructions of a physician" and subserving "him in his ministrations to the patient" when she administered the injection of tetracycline . . .

. . . The principal arguments of counsel for the plaintiffs and the Hospital are directed toward the question as to whether the doctrine of *respondeat superior* should be applied to the Hospital for the act of the Nurse. We have concluded that the rule of *respondeat superior* should be applied to the Hospital . . .

The doctrine of *respondeat superior* is grounded on firm principles of law and justice. Liability is the rule, immunity the exception. It is not too much to expect that those who serve and minister to members of the public should do so, as do all others, subject to that principle and within the obligation not to injure through carelessness.

Hospitals should, in short, shoulder the responsibilities borne by everyone else. There is no reason to continue their exemption from the universal rule of *respondeat superior*. The test should be, for these institutions, whether charitable or profit–making, as it is for every other employer, was the person who committed the negligent injury–producing act one of its employees, and, if he was, was he acting within the scope of his employment.

If we were to rule that *respondeat superior* does not apply because the hospital is not licensed as a Nurse, then it would seem to follow that an airline should not be liable for the negligence of its pilot because the airline is not licensed to fly an aircraft . . . The Hospital was the employer of the Nurse. Only it could assign the Nurse to certain hours, certain areas and certain patients. There was no choice in the Doctor or the plaintiffs as to the identity of the nurses who would serve Lisa. In this day and age a hospital should be responsible for the acts of its nurses within the scope of their employment, irrespective of whether they are acting "administratively" or "professionally" . . .

Some of the authorities mentioned, and others, make no distinction in application of the rule of *respondeat superior* to hospitals between employed nurses and employed doctors.

Expressly, this opinion relates only to nurses. Also, it should be borne in mind that this decision relates only to the case in which the nurse acts out of the presence of the doctor.

Plaintiffs, not too energetically, argue that the doctrine of *res ipsa loquitur* be applied against the Hospital. They cite cases from other jurisdictions in which the doctrine has been so applied, but no Colorado decision involving a hospital. It appears that usually when the doctrine is applied to a hospital, the cause of the injury is a mystery and there is a reasonable and logical inference that agents of the hospital were negligent and that such negligence caused the injury . . . Here, there is no uncertainty as to the cause of the injury. The plaintiffs, Hospital and Doctor concede that it resulted from the injection into or near the sciatic nerve. Under such circumstances the doctrine is not applicable . . .

There is now considered the order dismissing the complaint as against the Doctor. The Doctor was a private physician. He left orders at the Hospital for post-operative injections to be given by any nurse on the staff of the Hospital. The plaintiffs alleged in the complaint that the Nurse gave the injection "while acting pursuant to Defendant Aumiller's directions and while under his control and supervision." However, the Nurse stated in her answers to interrogations that she and Lisa were the only ones present in the room at the time of the injection and that Lisa's parents were standing just outside the room. The plaintiffs concede in their brief that the Doctor was not present at the time the injection was given.

A portion of the argument of the plaintiffs is that, since the trial court sustained the motion for summary judgment in favor of the Hospital because the act of the Nurse was a doctor-directed professional one, then the Doctor must be liable because he directed the performance of the professional act . . .

The Hospital in its brief has argued that the Doctor is liable because he ordered the injection . . .

It is apparent from the record that the Doctor did not have the control necessary to apply the doctrine of *respondeat superior* to him. He did not know what nurses would give the injection. The Nurse had been employed by the Hospital and was under its control and direction. The Doctor, not being present when the injection was given, had no opportunity to control its administration. His instructions that injections were to be given did not give rise to a master-servant relationship.

The Doctor's position here is vastly different from that . . . where it was held that in the operating room the surgeon is master, has the exclusive control of the acts of the orderly and nurse, and is responsible for their negligence during the time that the patient is in the operating room and the surgeon is present . . .

The last assignment of error relates to the order of the trial court denying the plaintiffs' motion for production by the Hospital of an "Incident Report" prepared by the Nurse. The Hospital objected to production of the document on the ground that it was prepared for the Hospital's attorney and was protected by attorney–client privilege. After the Nurse prepared the Incident Report a copy was placed in Lisa's hospital chart, another copy went to the Hospital Administrator and a further copy went to the Director of Nurses at the Hospital. At the time of the hearing on the motion to produce, the testimony of Mr. Frank A. Buchanan, a Boulder attorney, was taken. He testified, *inter alia*, to the following effect: He had been general counsel for the Hospital for about ten years, but was not representing the Hospital in this action. Incident reports were made at the Hospital, not only during the period of his representation, but prior thereto. He had not seen the Incident Report prepared by the Nurse in this matter and was not made aware of its contents until after this action was filed. He had seen incident reports from time to time as to "various things that occur at the hospital." He recalled two or three occasions. To see the incident report gave him "a basis for investigation of facts, to interview the doctor or interview people involved and on which, well, the incident report can give me information if there was some." He did not see all incident reports that were prepared.

Mr. Buchanan's answer to the question, "Do you know for whom these reports are made as a matter of course?" was as follows:

> Well, I know they are made for—one of the reasons for them is certainly for me to be able to advise; I suppose that an attorney is part of management and in that respect you could say that it is management, but in another sense an attorney is separate counsel, so I certainly advise management, and I certainly—this is certain information that is available to them. I can't answer with honesty as to the primary purpose of it. It certainly is a tool that I use, yes, sir.

A reminder was given to all nurses by the Hospital on October 7, 1963 as follows: Report any incident—no matter how small or unimportant it may seem—immediately to the Nurses Office, on an Incident Form, at least two copies. This includes any item lost, etc.

It may well be that the practice of making an incident report resulted from the advice of counsel, but it seems rather plain that these incident reports were not prepared for the attorney. Rather, they were prepared for certain administrative officials of the Hospital and they were available to the Hospital's attorney if he wished to see them. "To entitle the party to the protection accorded to privileged communications, the communications must have been made to the counsel, *attorney*, or solicitor acting, for the time being, in the character of legal adviser, and must be made by the client for the purpose of professional advice or aid upon the subject of his rights and liabilities." In our view the Court should have ordered the incident report to be produced, and now should do so . . . appropriately.

o **Recap of the Case.** The decision in *Bernardi* changes the law relating to *respondeat superior*. Prior to this decision, hospitals were not liable for all of the acts of nurses they employed. They were liable for the "administrative" aspects of nursing practice, but not "professional" acts of nurses on the theory that physicians were responsible for professional conduct since nurses acted only under doctors' orders. The court in *Bernardi* recognized the difficulties in drawing these distinctions. It also recognized that such distinctions no longer reflected the reality of nurses' roles. The court decided, therefore, that a hospital may be liable for only and all acts of nurses employed by the hospital.

5

Common Instances of Nursing Malpractice

There are a number of situations which occur repeatedly and often result in liability for nurses: 1) leaving foreign objects inside patients following surgery; 2) improper use of equipment; 3) improper exercise of nursing skills; 4) administration of an improper medication or solution; 5) failure to properly observe the patient; 6) failure to refuse to follow inappropriate orders; and 7) falls.

EMPLOYEES OF VETERANS' ADMINISTRATION HOSPITAL LIABLE FOR TOWEL LEFT IN PATIENT'S ABDOMEN DURING SURGERY

Leaving a foreign object inside the patient following surgery is a classic example of negligent conduct. Objects frequently left behind include needles and sponges. In at least one case, *Jefferson v. U.S.*, 77 F.Supp. 706 (D.Md. 1948), *aff'd*, 178 F.2d 518 (4th Cir. 1949), *aff'd* 340 U.S. 135 (1950), the operating personnel left an army towel inside the patient. It measured 2 1/2 feet long by 1 1/2 feet wide and bore the legend "Medical Department U.S. Army." The court decided that the towel was left in the plaintiff's stomach during an operation at Fort Belvoir and that those who participated were negligent.

Jefferson v. U.S., 77 F.Supp. 706 (D.Md. 1948)
United States District Court

The plaintiff who had been an aviation mechanic at the Glenn L. Martin Company's plant in Baltimore, enlisted in the United States Army October 22, 1942. On July 3, 1945 while still in the Army he underwent an abdominal operation for gall bladder trouble at Fort Belvoir, Virginia, a Government Hospital. The operation was performed by a United States Army medical officer who was the chief surgeon at the hospital at the time. The complaint in this case is that a large towel, 30 inches long by 18 inches wide, was negligently left in the plaintiff's abdomen during the operation and remained there until it was discovered during a subsequent abdominal operation performed at the Johns Hopkins Hospital in Baltimore on March 13, 1946. He alleges total permanent disability as a result of this alleged negligence.

The evidence established the following briefly summarized facts.

1. When the plaintiff first enlisted in the Army he was 45 years of age. He had previously had an abdominal operation for appendicitis from which he had apparently completely recovered. About five months after enlisting and while in the Army he had an abdominal operation at an Army hospital at Indiantown Gap, Pennsylvania, during which one of his kidneys was removed. After several weeks in the hospital he returned to service and was given somewhat lighter work at various aviation fields as a flight chief. From January 19 to May 17, 1943 he had various medical complaints diagnosed as hydronephrosis and a subsequent diagnosis of herpes of the lower lip reported cured on February 7, 1943; but on February 19, 1943 a further diagnosis indicated pleurisy, reported cured on March 3, 1943. From February to April 1945 he had an ill defined condition of the gastrointestinal system including vomiting, with non-functioning gall bladder and an absence of the right kidney which had been removed on March 5, 1943. From April 24 to November 20, 1945 he had cholecystitis. The operation on July 3, 1945, made the basis of the complaint in this case, was for cholecystostomy. During the earlier portion of this period he was at Edgewood, Maryland, suffering from jaundice for two or three months until he was sent to Fort Belvoir, Virginia.

2. The plaintiff is a naturalized citizen, a native of Denmark. He was honorably discharged from the Army on

January 9, 1946. On March 3, 1946 he went to the Johns Hopkins Hospital in Baltimore for treatment (because of vomiting spells and nausea which had commenced about two weeks prior to admission and grown increasingly more severe). On March 13, 1946 he was operated upon by Dr. Grose who had graduated at Johns Hopkins University Medical School some years previously, had been an interne there in the surgical department for a year or so; had served for two or three years in the Hopkins Medical Unit in the South Pacific, and had then returned to Hopkins for a while and at the particular time was engaged in private surgical practice.

3. Dr. Grose found a well healed medical scar on the front abdomen of the plaintiff through which he again operated and as a result of the operation found a towel in the lower part of the plaintiff's stomach which had partly worked into the duodenum. This towel was removed, measured and photographed. It bore the legend "Medical Department U.S. Army". It was 2 1/2 feet long by 1 1/2 feet wide. Dr. Grose also found the condition and relation of the plaintiff's stomach and intestines to each other was such as to indicate very clearly that there had been a previous operation on the plaintiff for gastrojejunostomy which, in Dr. Grose's opinion, meant an opening of the stomach. The doctor expressed the opinion that there were three possibilities as to how the towel could have gotten into the plaintiff's stomach. First (theoretical largely) that it had been swallowed by the plaintiff; second, that it had been left in the plaintiff's abdomen during a surgical operation which must have occurred some months before, which, if it did not involve an opening of the stomach and placing of the towel therein, had resulted in the towel working its way through the walls of the stomach into the stomach itself (and then partially back into the duodenum). While this was a possibility by reason of some few prior recorded cases of a similar nature, such a happening would be very rare indeed; third the remaining possibility was that in a prior operation, as for instance, gastrojejunostomy, the towel had been placed in the stomach to prevent the flow of matter from the intestines into the stomach and had been inadvertently left in the stomach when the patient's abdominal surgical wound was closed.

4. After the operation by Dr. Grose the plaintiff was subsequently treated at the Marine Hospital in Baltimore, medically and surgically. He was later examined by Dr. Grose and found to have sustained a serious hernia which was attributed by Dr. Grose to the after effects of the operation at

Hopkins thought to have been caused by inflammation or infection as a post–operative result of the towel.

5. The present physical condition of the plaintiff is that he gets some relief from the effects of the hernia by wearing a corset. He is able to walk about and stand around but cannot well lean forward either standing or sitting in a chair. After three or four hours of any activity he finds it necessary to rest, preferably by lying down. In Dr. Grose's opinion he is not employable industrially but could do clerical work if otherwise qualified therefor. As the plaintiff is nearly 50 years of age and a mechanic by prior occupation, it is doubtful if he could engage in any gainful employable pursuit.

6. The Army Hospital at Ft. Belvoir, Virginia, is a regional hospital with a large staff of hospital employees and with numerous patients in different wards. The Chief Surgeon at the hospital at that time, is now in private practice in New York City. He testified as a witness for the government that the operation at Ft. Belvoir upon the plaintiff had been conducted by himself; that he recalled the case of the plaintiff for two reasons (1) that the plaintiff was an older man than most of the Army patients and (2) because the plaintiff spoke English imperfectly. He did not recall in precise detail all the incidents of the particular operation but stated definitely that the operation was for cholecystostomy, which involved no opening of the stomach and that in fact he had never performed (the operation of) gastrojejunostomy while he was in the Army service. He had been in private practice specializing as a surgeon for some ten years or more before entering the Army where he saw service in Africa and Italy before being appointed as Chief Surgeon at Ft. Belvoir. He is a graduate of recognized medical schools and a lecturer on surgery in one of them. He referred to a recorded account of the operation dictated by him to a secretary and signed by him shortly after the operation had been performed on the plaintiff, in accordance with the customary requirements of the Army. This account of the operation showed that it was for cholecystostomy which did not involve gastrojejunostomy requiring an opening of the stomach. He said that the original purpose of the operation was to remove the gall bladder but he found upon examination that it was located in such a way that this was impossible and therefore he substituted for the removal of the gall bladder the insertion of a drain. The operation including the administration of the anesthetic lasted about four hours, and after the operation the patient was placed in an oxygen tent. He was not sure of the length of the incision that was made.

Ordinarily such an operation would require only a three-inch incision. This particular one might possibly have required more. He did not use any towels such as that later found in the plaintiff's stomach although such ordinary hand and face towels were doubtless in the operating room. Such towels and bandages as were used were attached to metal clips to insure facility of removal after the operation and if one had inadvertently been left in the opening it would have been discovered by an X-ray. His attention was not again called to the particular operation until a few months ago when he received a letter of inquiry from the Army stating that suit had been filed by the plaintiff based on an operation at Ft. Belvoir while he was Chief Surgeon there. The suit was filed July 31, 1947. The government did not call as witnesses any other members of the hospital staff either assistant surgeons or nurses some of whom must have been present during the operation. The Assistant United States Attorney stated that he was unable to ascertain who they were so long after the operation.

7. A few days after the plaintiff's honorable discharge from the Army he filed a formal application for service-connected disability with the Veterans' Administration. On March 11, 1946 the plaintiff was allowed 30% disability for the removal of the kidney while in the Army, in the amount of a monthly payment of $34.50. Later, consequent upon further regular physical examinations, after the removal of the towel from the plaintiff's stomach and his subsequent increased disability, his disability rate was increased on October 16, 1947 so that he now has for some time past been receiving monthly checks for $138 as 100% disability. In all he has received to date as of April 30, $3,645.50, and on estimated life expectancy of 22 years under existing legislation, will prespectively receive $31,947 in addition. The original disability allowance of $34.50 was fixed by statute as the amount payable for the removal of one kidney. The increase in the allowance was in the discretion and judgment of the Veterans' Administration. By stipulation of the parties life expectancy of the plaintiff at his present age, based on ordinary average mortality tables, is 22 years. His earning capacity at the Martin plant had been about $1.30 an hour with some reasonable expectation of advancement if the plaintiff had been able to return to work in the usual way. The commuted value of this earning capacity for an estimated life expectancy of 22 years would be about $45,000.

From the evidence as a whole, despite the factual difficulties and uncertainties, I conclude that the facts justify the finding that the towel must have been placed in the plaintiff's abdomen or stomach at the time of the operation at Ft. Belvoir as alleged; and the failure to remove it before closing the surgical wound was negligence on the part of agents or employees of the government at the hospital. There was no evidence of any abdominal operation on the plaintiff other than those mentioned; and it is highly improbable that the towel could have been left in the plaintiff at the time of the kidney operation.

I conclude also that if the plaintiff is entitled to recover at all in this case the actual and prospective payments made to him by the Veterans' Administration must be, as conceded by plaintiff's counsel, treated as diminution of the amount of the verdict; and in view of all the evidence in the case, including the plaintiff's various medical and surgical disabilities preceding the operation at Ft. Belvoir, I would conclude that presently a sum of $7,500 would be an appropriate verdict . . .

As previously indicated, the case is a difficult one on the facts as well as on the law. The nature of the suit is a typical one for professional malpractice; but nevertheless the facts of the particular case are quite unusual and the conclusion which I have reached on the facts that there was negligence proximately resulting in damage to the plaintiff is not free from all doubt. However, . . . I will not unduly prolong discussion of the facts because, although they are unusual, after all it is merely a fact question to be determined by the court without a jury. The plaintiff is not obliged to prove the fact beyond a reasonable doubt, but only by a preponderance of the evidence. To establish the negligence plaintiff's counsel relies strongly upon the common law doctrine or rule of *res ipsa loquitur*. It is conceded by counsel on both sides that the rule applies in proper cases both under the Virginia and Maryland decisions and my attention has not been directed to any important difference between the two States with respect to the application of the rule to the instant case.

But the rule itself is only one from which after proof of the main fact alleged by the plaintiff, the trier of facts is permitted to infer negligence in the absence of a sufficient exculpatory explanation by the defendant. In this case the fact alleged by the plaintiff is the negligent failure of the defendant to remove a towel from his abdomen or stomach which had been placed there in the course of surgical operation on July 3, 1945 at Ft. Belvoir, Virginia. There is no direct proof of this particular fact alleged and the rule of *res ipsa loquitur* would not of itself be sufficient to prove the fact as well as the inference of negligence. However, on the evidence as a whole, I have found as a fact that the towel must have been placed or left in the plaintiff's body at Ft. Belvoir, Virginia. And having thus found this fact the rule justifies the inference that there must have been negligence in leaving the towel in the plaintiff's body, in the absence of any convincing evidence of the lack of negligence in doing so. The only evidence submitted by the defendant was to the effect that no towel was used in the operation. Of course if the trier of facts so found, that would be an end of the plaintiff's case. But as I have felt obliged to reject this conclusion of fact, I must treat the case as one where the fact has been proved and there is no explanation by the defendant of how the very unusual fact occurred.

For the reasons stated, I have concluded that the complaint must be dismissed . . .

o **Recap of the Case.** In this case, a towel was left in the patient's abdomen during surgery. After this fact was established, the court determined that this act was a negligent one. The principles of this case are still applicable today. Courts routinely conclude that allowing foreign objects to remain in a patient constitutes negligent conduct. Expert testimony is rarely required to prove such negligence since this is a type of situation within the understanding of non-physicians.

NURSE NOT LIABLE FOR DEFECT IN CLAMP

The rules governing improper use of equipment are summarized in *Butler v. Northwestern Hospital*, 202 Minn. 290, 278 N.W.37 (1938). If nurses are aware that equipment is faulty, they have a duty to refuse to utilize the equipment. If the fault in the equipment is not readily apparent, nurses will not be found liable for the results of its use.

The doctor in *Butler* ordered a proctoclysis, a method by which a solution is introduced drop by drop into the body for nourishment. The nurse gathered what she thought was all of the appropriate equipment for this procedure. After putting hot water into this partially-assembled apparatus, she realized that the equipment she had was inadequate. Prior to leaving the room to obtain the correct equipment, she placed the end of the tube on the patient's bed and secured it with a spring clamp to prevent leakage of hot water. The clamp came off and hot water flowed onto the patient's bed, severely burning his legs. The patient did not feel the water because he was still numb from the waist down from anesthesia administered during surgery.

The patient subsequently sued the hospital. He also attempted to hold the nurse responsible for his injuries, but the court refused to hold her responsible because she did not notice any defect in the clamp.

Butler v. Northwestern Hospital,
202 Minn. 290, 278 N.W. 37 (1938)
Supreme Court of Minnesota

. . . November 2, 1935, plaintiff, 74 years of age, underwent an appendicitis operation at defendant hospital. That afternoon, while plaintiff was undergoing the operation, arrangements were made in his behalf for a special nurse to attend him after the operation. Following the usual practice, the hospital notified the nurses' central registering bureau (an organization which keeps a list of registered nurses and furnishes such when requested by hospitals) and procured the professional services of Mrs. Nordgren, a duly registered nurse, and an alumnus of defendant's Hospital Training School. She reported for duty about 6:15. Plaintiff was brought from the operating room shortly thereafter. In the meantime, she had learned from the anesthetist that the operating surgeon wanted plaintiff to be given a "tap water" proctoclysis. That is a method by which a solution is introduced into the body drop by drop through the rectum for nourishment. The "tap water" wanted and ordered was plain water heated to 120 degrees Fahrenheit. Equipment necessary for a proctoclysis consists of a container, a standard or stand which supports the container above the level of the bed, a rubber tube, a Murphy drip, which is a glass coupling used to enable the nurse to count the drip flow, a catheter (i.e., a rectal tube), and a screw clamp placed on the rubber tubing to regulate the flow. The equipment provided for and placed in plaintiff's room consisted of a container, a rubber rectal tube, and a spring clamp. These were among a collection of articles in a tray on the table. Mrs. Nordgren secured a standard and attempted to construct out of these articles the apparatus for proctoclysis. She filled the can with hot water and hitched it to the standard. Realizing then that the equipment was inadequate, she placed the end of the rubber tubing on the bed and went out to secure the other necessary articles. Before leaving plaintiff's bedside she fastened the spring clamp on the tubing to prevent any flow. In her absence the clamp came apart, allowing the hot water to drain from the container through the rubber tubing and onto plaintiff's bed (provided with a rubber sheet) so that his back and thighs were severely scalded. Because of a spinal anesthetic, plaintiff was insensitive from the waist down. He did not realize what happened other than that he was warm.

Plaintiff seeks to hold defendant liable on the theory that it furnished a defective spring clamp, which, because of its defective condition, caused plaintiff's injury. That is the determinative issue here. Any question of Mrs. Nordgren's agency was foreclosed by the court's charge, that "the defendant cannot be held liable for any act or omission of the special nurse, Susanna Nordgren." That is the law of the case; hence the nurse must be considered as plaintiff's agent or servant. Defendant's liability, if any, must rest entirely upon the claimed breach of duty in failing to furnish an efficient clamp, and that such failure proximately resulted in plaintiff's injuries.

1. It is well established that one who furnishes an instrumentality for a special use or service impliedly warrants the article furnished to be reasonably fit and suitable for the purpose for which it is expressly let out, or for which, from its character, he must be aware it is intended to be used and is liable for injuries to the bailee or third persons for injuries proximately resulting from any defect due to his want of due care.

2. Assuming, as we must, that the nurse was plaintiff's agent or servant, it follows that the involved clamp and other articles present in plaintiff's room were furnished by defendant to be used for customarily needed purposes where an important surgical operation has been performed. That, obviously, was the intention. And the articles so selected by defendant had to be reasonably fit therefor. Defendant's argument that "the clamp was not furnished by the hospital for use in treatment of the plaintiff" is unavailing. It is not enough to say that the purpose of the articles in the room was "unknown and unexplained." The arrangement with the hospital could mean nothing less than the furnishing of necessary facilities and equipment for the efficient operation of its business. And these must necessarily be furnished for the particular purpose for which they are needed and designed.

3. It is strongly urged that this equipment, among which was the defective spring clamp, was not furnished for use in

proctoclysis. The effect of that argument is that since the use made was other than that intended, injuries arising therefrom are not attributable to any fault of defendant. With that we cannot agree. It is true, as appears from the record, that that kind of clamp is ordinarily utilized in the administration of an enema where the purpose is to allow either a full flow of the solution or to cut it off altogether. A spring clamp is ideally adapted to that purpose. On the other hand, in proctoclysis the solution is injected drop by drop, a result which can be had only by the use of a screw clamp which can be adjusted to increase or decrease the flow, or shut it off completely. But the important thing as regards the intended use of the clamp is not the general treatment that is given, but rather, and only, the particular function of the clamp in any treatment, i.e., its general use which is to shut off liquid flow through rubber tubing. Our thought is best expressed in the very words of defendant's counsel: "Our attention here is directed at one small item of that equipment, a single clamp which is used to shut off the stream of flow through rubber tubing. It is common knowledge that rubber tubing is used about a hospital for a number of purposes not necessarily limited to the treatment of patients. The use of the type of clamp involved is not restricted to hospitals. The same clamps are often used in homes, industry and laboratories, in fact, wherever rubber tubing is used." It would seem, therefore, that defendant should be held to be aware of the obvious nature of its use, which is the stoppage of the flow of a solution through a rubber tube conduit. And that is so irrespective of the particular treatment being given. From this it follows, also, that defendant may be held liable for injuries proximately resulting from the defective condition of the clamp of which it had or with reasonable care could have acquired knowledge . . .

There is sufficient sustaining evidence to show that the clamp was discoverably defective. It consists of two parts, a body or base and the lever above. The nurse, her brother, and husband testified that the two sides of the body of the clamp, each containing one hole through which the ends of the lever were inserted for attachment, had come apart, releasing the lever and the tongue or clamping part from the base or body part of the clamp. The effect of the verdict in plaintiff's behalf establishes defendant's negligence. From the evidence we are not prepared to say, as a matter of law, that defendant could not readily have discovered this defect if a reasonable inspection thereof had been made.

4. There is intimation by defendant that the injury was caused by the negligent conduct of the nurse. Her negligence, if any, can be considered only in relation to the defective clamp. No other is material . . . Mrs. Nordgren, although a trained professional, could reasonably rely upon the hospital's furnishing a proper clamp. We agree with defendant that if the article furnished was obviously unfit for the use for which it was furnished and intended, and the nurse used it in violation of the usual standards of due care of nursing practice, the defendant cannot be chargeable with any injurious effects therefrom . . . But the defect was not patent. The clamp was furnished apparently ready for use, and it was not her duty to examine into its mechanical parts for the discovery of possible defects . . . The defect was not discovered until she returned from her effort to get the missing proctoclysis equipment, and she then found it apart.

5. Proximate cause is oftentimes a difficult problem to solve . . . "As a practical matter, legal responsibility must be limited to those causes which are so close to the result, or of such significance as causes, that the law is justified in imposing liability. This limitation is not a matter of causation, it is one of policy; and the attempt to state it in terms of causation can lead to nothing but confusion." In the instant case we think there can be no serious question but that defendant's negligence "as a practical matter" was so close to plaintiff's harm as to justify the jury in finding liability. Was, then, the negligence, if such there be, on the part of the nurse a sufficient intervening cause to compel the triers of fact to relieve defendant of that responsibility?

6. "Intervening forces introduce a further problem, as to whether defendant is to be relieved from liability for an injury to which he has in fact contributed, by a superseding cause for which he is not responsible. 'Intervening force' is one which comes into active operation in producing the result, after the defendant's negligence. 'Intervening' is used in a time sense; it refers to later events. Conditions existing and forces already in operation at the time of defendant's conduct are not included within the term."

7. The verdict is assailed as excessive . . . He suffered genuine torment. True, he is getting along in years and perhaps has not much time left during which he must bear this suffering. But we are not persuaded that the verdict can be assailed upon this ground. His remaining days, that should be for him, as for all normal persons, the eventide of life's happiest moments, he must now endure in pain.

The order is affirmed.

o **Recap of the Case.** The patient was burned by hot water when a defective clamp, which had been carefully closed by the nurse apparently malfunctioned. The patient attempted to hold both the hospital and the nurse liable for his injuries. The court agreed that the hospital was liable, but refused to hold the nurse responsible as well. The court determined that the equipment used by the nurse which injured the patient appeared to be safe. The nurse was correct to rely upon this appearance. She was not required to take it apart to examine it for malfunctioning parts. She would have been liable only if the equipment was obviously defective and she used it anyway, thereby causing injury to the patient.

SUPERVISORY NURSE LIABLE FOR OVERDOSE RESULTING IN PATIENT'S DEATH

Liability for improper exercise of nursing skills and administration of an improper medication are illustrated by *Norton v. Argonaut Insurance Company*, 144 So.2d 249 (La.Ct.App. 1962). In this case, a nurse incorrectly administered medication intravenously instead of orally. The patient died as a result, and the nurse was held liable for her conduct.

There are a number of practical lessons for nurses in this case. First, the patient's mother was permitted to continue to administer the child's medication while the child was in the hospital. This practice created confusion and uncertainty and, at the very least, contributed significantly to the environment in which the fatal accident occurred. Nurses must never allow patients to administer their own medication or relatives to give medication to patients. Second, the nurse who injected the patient had been in a supervisory position for several years immediately prior to this incident and had not practiced "hands on" care for some time. Consequently, she was unaware that the medication ordered was available in a liquid form. Nurses should be aware of their limits and should not practice unless their skills are current. Finally, the defendant nurse was uncertain about what the physician's order meant. She had a legal duty to clarify the order before administering the medication. This duty applies to all nurses. Whenever orders are unclear, nurses must take steps to clarify them.

Norton v. Argonaut Insurance Company
144 So.2d 249 (La.Ct. App. 1962)

. . . The sequence of events which culminated in the unfortunate and untimely demise of plaintiffs' infant daughter commenced shortly after the child's birth on September 29, 1959. Dr. Charles N. Bombet, the Norton's pediatrician, examined Robyn the day of her birth and attended her subsequently. At birth the child appeared normal but approximately two months thereafter she commenced to exhibit symptoms which prompted the mother to take her to Dr. Bombet for further examination. In early December, 1959, Dr. Bombet detected loud heart murmurs which indicated to him that the child was afflicted with congenital heart disease. At Dr. Bombert's suggestion, Dr. John B. Stotler, Cardiologist, and Dr. Charles Beskin, a specialist in heart surgery, were called in consultation. After examination, Doctors Stotler, Beskin and Bombet, in consultation, agreed that in all probability heart surgery was indicated to correct the congenital deformity noted. It was further agreed that prior to final determination regarding the proposed surgery, additional examination was desirable. With this view in mind, Dr. Stotler admitted the child to Baton Rouge General Hospital December 15, 1959 to conduct further tests and examinations deemed desirable under the circumstances.

On December 15, 1959, Dr. Stotler entered on the physician's order sheet (a hospital form whereon is noted and recorded the doctor's orders and instructions relative to medication and treatment to be given the patient) orders for various drugs including, inter alia, the following:

"Elixir Pediatric Lanoxin 2.5 cc (o.125 mg) q6h X 3 then once daily"

It is conceded by all parties that the foregoing order for medication meant that the patient was to be administered 2.5 ccs of the prescribed drug (known by the trade or brand name of "Lanoxin") every six hours for three doses and once daily thereafter.

There is no dispute that Elixir Pediatrix Lanoxin (hereinafter referred to simply as "Lanoxin") is in reality a derivate of digitalis and that because of its potency it is poisonous if administered in overdoses, therefore, it is to be used with caution and care. It is prescribed in the treatment of certain types of cardiac or heart patients. Briefly stated, the function of the drug is to increase the efficiency or strength of the pumping action of the heart while at the same time reducing the pulse thereby minimizing strain on that most vital organ. In the instant case, it appears that not only was the child's heart congenitally defective but also that her pulse rate was 140. According to the record the medicine comes in three forms namely 1) elixir or in alcohol solution which is administered orally or by mouth by means of a calibrated medicine dropper which is supplied with each bottle of the elixir; 2) pill or tablet form (somewhat similar to the common aspirin) which is likewise taken orally; and 3) injectible liquid form which is contained in sealed ampules containing two cubic centimers each of the solution and which is administered by injection or hypodermic needle.

There is no dispute among the medical experts who testified herein that a patient who is placed on digitalis must first be "digitalized" which in lay language means the administration of a series of doses (usually three or four) given at intervals of six hours to accustom the patient to the drug and simultaneously attain a desired reaction. When, in the opinion of the attending physician, the patient has been properly digitalized, the patient is then placed on a single daily dose which is referred to in the medical profession as a "maintenance dose" and which, in the absence of an emergency, is administered in oral form.

The manufacturer's recommended dosage for children up to 10 years of age is 0.01 milligrams per pound of body weight every six hours during the digitalization process followed by a daily maintenance dose equal to 0.01 milligrams of the drug per pound of body weight once daily or in divided doses. It is conceded that the daily maintenance dose for the Norton infant was approximately 0.11 considering the record shows that she weighed almost 11 pounds. It likewise appears that in the elixir form 1 cubic centimeter of the elixir contains 0.05 milligrams of digitalis, whereas the injectible type contains 0.25 milligrams per cubic centimeter. The term milligram is employed to indicate the amount of digitalis in either preparation whereas the term cubic centimeter or c.c. denotes merely the volume of the solution in which the drug is contained. From the foregoing it is evident that 3 c.cs. of the elixir contain only 0.15 milligrams whereas 3 c.cs. of the injectible solution contain 0.75 milligrams or five times as much drug. It is conceded that some discretion is permitted the prescribing physician in deviating from or exceeding the manufacturer's recommended dosages dependent upon results achieved with a particular patient. While the exact dosage which the child should have received according to the manufacturer's recommendation was slightly less than 2.5 c.cs. of the elixir, since the child's weight was approximately 11 pounds and 2.5 c.cs. of the elixir contains 0.12 1/2 c.cs., it is acknowledged by all the medical experts that neither the 2.5 c.cs. prescribed by Dr. Stotler as the daily maintenance dose nor the 3 c.cs. prescribed January 2, 1960, for one dose only was excessive or would have in any way harmed the child if administered in the elixir form. There is, however, some dispute among the medical experts regarding the effect of a double dose of 3 c.cs. of the elixir administered within a period of approximately one hour. All the experts agree, however, that 3 c.cs. administered intramuscularly is a fatal overdose for a 3 month old infant as was most tragically demonstrated in the case at bar.

The principle difference between the route selected for administration of the drug, that is, whether it be given orally or by injection, appears to be the reaction time or time in which it is absorbed by the system and the patient begins to derive benefit therefrom. Almost immediate results are obtained by intravenous injection (injection directly into the veins) for the reason that the medication is inducted directly into the blood stream. The slowest route is by way of mouth for the medication must first be absorbed or assimilated by the blood stream and then carried through the body. Intramuscular injection (injection into a muscle) though slower than the intravenous route is more rapid than oral administration. It further appears with reasonable certainty that taken orally the drug loses some of its potency in the process of being absorbed into the blood stream and that 0.15 milligrams of the oral form (elixir or tablet) will not produce quite as much net result or effect on the patient as 0.15 given intramuscularly.

The third of the three digitalization doses ordered by Dr. Stotler on December 15, 1959 was not timely administered by the nursing staff whereupon Mrs. Norton who remained with her child while the infant was in the sanitarium, became concerned and requested and was granted permission by Dr. Stotler to thereafter administer the daily maintenance dose of 2.5 c.c. which Dr. Stotler prescribed. Dr. Stotler instructed Mrs. Norton in the use of the calibrated medicine dropper by means of which the medicine is administered and thereafter Mrs. Norton herself gave the medication daily.

The child was discharged from the hospital December 16, 1959, and returned home to await the scheduling of the surgery which was to be performed soon thereafter.

On December 28, 1959, Dr. Bombet found on examination that the child's condition had apparently worsened. He noted that the baby had a cough, was feverish and appeared to be losing weight. Since the medication then being administered did not appear to be improving the child to any extent, he considered it necessary to return the infant to the hospital the following day and consequently, on December 29, 1959, Dr. Bombet readmitted the child to the hospital. On this occasion he issued admission orders on the infant to be placed in the child's hospital chart or record. Included in his admission orders were instructions regarding medication, diet, etc., and the notation that special medication was being administered by the mother. In this connection it appears that Mrs. Norton preferred to continue administration of the daily maintenance dose of the Lanoxin herself since she had been performing this function since the child's initial admission to the hopsital on December 15th. Dr. Bombet noted in the hospital admission orders of December 29, 1959, that special medication was being given by the mother to thusly advise the hospital staff and employees that some medication was being administered the child other than that which he placed on the order sheet and would, therefore, be administered by the hospital nursing staff.

On January 2, 1960 (Saturday) Dr. Stotler examined the Norton baby at approximately noon while in the course of making his rounds in the hospital. As a result of this examination he concluded that the child needed an increase in the daily maintenance dose of Lanoxin and instructed Mrs. Norton, who was present in the room, to increase the daily dose of the Lanoxin for that day only to 3 c.cs. instead of the usual 2.5 c.cs. Following this instruction to Mrs. Norton, Dr. Stotler went to the nurse's station in the hospital pediatric unit floor to check the hospital chart or record on the Norton infant and noted on the Doctor's Order Sheet contained therein certain instructions among which only the following is pertinent to the issues involved herein: "Give 3.0 cc. Lanoxin today for 1 dose only".

Dr. Stotler's entry of the foregoing order for medication constitutes the basis of plaintiff's claim against Aetna as the professional liability insurer of Dr. Stotler. It is frankly conceded by Aetna that unless Dr. Stotler indicated on the order sheet that he had instructed the patient's mother to increase the daily maintenance dose of Lanoxin to 3.0 c.cs. and administer the medication, his entry of the aforesaid prescription on the order sheet would indicate that the nursing staff of the hospital was to give the medication prescribed. It is further conceded that under such circumstances the child was subjected to the possibility of being administered a second dose of Lanoxin. The possibility thus presented is exactly what occurred in the instant case. A member of the nursing staff noting Dr. Stotler's orders to administer the 3 c.cs. of Lanoxin for one dose only administered 3 c.cs. of lanoxin in its injectible form instead of the elixir form which Dr. Stotler intended. The importance of this difference in the form of the medication has hereinbefore been shown. It is readily conceded by all concerned that the 3 c.cs. of Lanoxin administered the baby by hypodermic was a lethal overdose and was in fact the cause of the infant's demise.

The salient issue in the instant case is whether or not the order for Lanoxin as written by Dr. Stotler on the order sheet under date of January 2, 1960, indicated that the Lanoxin should be administered orally (as the child had been administered this medication in the past) or whether his instruction as worded indicated that the injectible form of Lanoxin would be given hypodermically. In this connection it is desired to state that both the elixir and injectible form of Lanoxin are measured in terms of cubic centimeters. The positions of the respective defendants may be stated as follows: Mrs. Evans, (the registered nurse who administered the fatal dose), and Argonaut maintain that the failure of Dr. Stotler to designate the route of administration was responsible for administration of injectible Lanoxin instead of elixir orally because the order as written indicated the route to be intramuscularly by hypodermic. On the other hand, Dr. Stotler's insurer, Aetna, contends in substance that the order was written according to the custom and practice of other physicians in the same field in the same locality and that in the event of any uncertainty concerning the order, it was the duty of the hospital employees to make sufficient inquiry to determine which type of administration was intended.

It is readily admitted by Dr. Stotler in his testimony appearing in the record that he was in error in failing to note on the order sheet that the 3 c.cs. of Lanoxin ordered January 2, 1960, for one dose only, had already been given by the mother or was to be administered by her because, without such explanation it was the duty of the hospital nursing staff to administer the medication. Aetna maintains, however, that this admitted oversight on the part of its insured subjected the infant to the possibility of a double oral dose only which would not have been fatal. In this regard, Aetna advances the following arguments: 1) The order as written meant and intended that the drug prescribed be given orally by mouth for the reason that it is the custom, practice and understanding in hospitals in the community that drugs prescribed on a hospital order sheet are to be administered orally or by mouth unless otherwise indicated by the doctor prescribing same; 2) In the event of ambiguity or uncertainty regarding medication prescribed it is the duty of the nurse administering the drug to call the attending physician for the purpose of clarification which admittedly was not done by the nurse who administered the fatal dose; and 3) That purpose and effect of Lanoxin is so well known to the medical and nursing professions it is inconceivable that any registered nurse would interpret an order thusly written to call for administration of what should be readily recognized as a lethal dose for a 3 month old infant, consequently such gross negligence on the part of the nurse in question constitutes an independent intervening cause relieving the physician of all liability. Stated otherwise, it is contended on behalf of Aetna that such gross negligence on the part of Nurse Evans is so incomprehensible, unforeseeable and inconceivable as to render the negligence of Dr. Stotler, if any, a remote rather than a proximate cause of the child's death.

The date of the tragedy with which we are here concerned, namely, January 2, 1960, was a Saturday. The nurse in charge of the pediatric unit, Miss Joan Walsh, a Registered Nurse, was absent from the hospital because it was her day off. The pediatric unit was in charge of Miss Barbara Jean Sipes, a Registered Nurse, who was assisted by a nurse's aid. Mrs. Florence Evans, Assistant Director of Nursing Service was the Senior Nurse on duty at the hospital at the time and in such capacity, exercised complete supervision and control of all nurses. Her duties were primarily administrative and supervisory. However, the rules of the institution required that when necessary she render assistance to the nurses on duty and perform routine nursing services. In addition, in the course of checking the operation of the numerous departments and units of the hospital (making the rounds, as it is referred to) Mrs. Evans went to the pediatric unit sometime after the lunch hour and discovered that the only Registered Nurse on duty, Miss Sipes, was quite busy with an emergency patient brought to the hospital and being attended by a Dr. Ruiz. Observing that the pediatric unit was in need of additional nurses under the circumstances shown, Mrs. Evans summoned a senior student nurse, Miss Meadows, to the pediatric unit from another department, and Mrs. Evans herself remained in the unit for a time. In checking the charts of the patients on the unit, Mrs.

Evans noted the order which Dr. Stotler had that day previously entered on the chart of the Norton baby including the prescription for 3 c.cs. of Lanoxin for one dose only.

The evidence discloses that although Mrs. Evans is a registered nurse with many years' experience it also appears that for the past several years her employment as a nurse has been principally in an administrative or supervisory capacity. It further appears that although Lanoxin in elixir preparation (in which form it can only be administered orally) had been available for a number of years, Mrs. Evans was not aware that the drug was manufactured in solution to be given orally. Because she had not practiced nursing as such for the past few years her knowledge of and familiarity with the drug in question was limited to the medicine as an injectible to be given only by hypodermic needle.

Noting that Dr. Stotler had ordered 3 c.cs. Lanoxin be given the Norton infant in one dose for that day only and knowing that it was the duty of the nursing staff to administer the medication, Mrs. Evans made inquiry and learning that the prescribed drug had not been administered decided to give the medication herself. She at no time considered administration of the drug other than by injection since by her own admission she was not then aware that Lanoxin came in elixir form. However, despite her limited knowledge of the drug, her training and womanly intuition warned her that 3 c.cs. of Lanoxin given by injection to a 3 month old infant appeared to be a rather large dose. She discussed the matter very briefly with the student nurse, Miss Meadows, and inquired of the Registered Nurse, Miss Sipes, whether or not the child had previously received Lanoxin. Mrs. Evans then examined the patient's hospital chart and found nothing therein which indicated the child had been receiving Lanoxin while in the hospital. In this regard, however, her testimony is vigorously disputed by defendant Aetna. Considering administration of the drug only by hypodermic needle, Mrs. Evans, accompanied by the Student Nurse, Miss Meadows, went to the medicine room of the pediatric unit and obtained two ampules of Lanoxin each containing 2 c.cs. of drug in its injectible form. While pondering the advisability of thusly administering what she considered to be a large dose, Mrs. Evans noted that Dr. Beskin, one of the consultants on the child's case, had entered the pediatric ward so Mrs. Evans consulted him about the matter and was advised that if Dr. Stotler prescribed 3 c.cs. he meant 3 c.cs. Still not certain about the matter Mrs. Evans also discussed the subject with Dr. Ruiz and was informed by him in effect that although the dose was the maximum dose, that if the doctor had prescribed that amount she could give it. The foregoing inquiry having satisfied Mrs. Evans' suspicions about the matter, Mrs. Evans then obtained a syringe, extracted 3 c.cs. of the medicine from the two ampules and injected one–half thereof into each buttock of the child. Following the injection Mrs. Evans noted on the chart that she administered the drug intramuscularly at 1:30 P.M. The injections upset the baby causing her to cry. Mrs. Norton then requested a hot water bottle to place on the baby's buttocks to alleviate the pain occasioned by the injections and was advised that such could not be obtained without the orders of the attending physician. Mrs. Norton then called Dr. Stotler and in the course of the conversation mentioned that the child had received additional medication by injection. Dr. Stotler immediately called the nurses' station of the pediatric unit and upon learning of the administration of the lethal dose of injectible Lanoxin issued emergency orders and summoned Doctors Bombet and Beskin. Despite all emergency measures, including opening the child's chest and massaging her heart, the infant died at 2:45 P.M., approximately one hour and 15 minutes following the fatal injection.

Except as hereinafter noted, the above recitation of the chronology of event culminating in this litigation is, in the main, undisputed. There are some areas of disagreement between the witnesses and contending parties as hereinafter noted.

Mrs. Florence Evans, a Registered Nurse with many years' experience and highly regarded by members of her own and the medical profession, testified that for the past number of years she has held mostly executive and administrative or supervisory positions in numerous hospitals including the Baton Rouge General Hospital. In such capacity most of her services are performed in the nursing service office rather than on the floor at a nursing station although she does incidentally perform nursing services while in the course of making her rounds in a supervisory capacity as occurred on the day of the accident in question.

By her own admission Mrs. Evans on the day in question was the Senior Nurse on duty and, as such, in complete charge and control of all nurses in the institution. She likewise frankly admits that she was not familiar with all forms of the drug Lanoxin and while acquainted with the medicine in a general way she was not aware that it came in elixir form and so far as she knew Lanoxin was prepared only as an injectible. Mrs.

Evans frankly conceded that at no time did she consider any route of administration other than by hypodermic needle. Both she and certain other nurses who testified stated that they were of the impression that drugs measured in cubic centimeters were intended to be given by injection. It occurring to her that 3 c.cs. appeared to be a rather large dose she made the inquiries herein previously noted. Her version, however, as to her conversations with Drs. Beskin and Ruiz do not accord with that of said doctors. According to Mrs. Evans while she was considering the dosage, Dr. Beskin entered the pediatric unit and sat at the table where the charts are kept. She stated that accompanied by the Student Nurse, Miss Meadows, she took the two ampules of injectible Lanoxin which she had secured from the medicine room, placed them and the chart on the table before Dr. Beskin and inquired, "Does he really mean to give this", or words to that effect whereupon Dr. Beskin replied: "If that's what he said, that's what he meant to give." Mrs. Evans then turned and walked toward the nearby medicine room where she encountered Dr. Ruiz who had come in with a patient. She handed Dr. Ruiz one of the ampules she carried and asked him about the dosage. According to Mrs. Evans, Dr. Ruiz responded that "it is a large dose". She then asked Dr. Ruiz if he would give this dose to a small child to which he replied "I suppose I would." She denied that the doctor's progress notes which appear on the child's chart and which indicated the child was on oral Lanoxin was in the record at the time. In this connection she testified that such notes are dictated by the attending physician into a recording machine in the hospital room and are typed and placed in the record after the patient's discharge. She likewise denied that the order sheet on the child's prior admission was in the record. According to Mrs. Evans nothing in the chart or record indicated to her that an oral route was intended.

Dr. Beskin testified that when Mrs. Evans consulted him about the dosage to be given the child he had no idea she intended administering the drug by injection. He was familiar with the fact that the child was on maintenance digitalis and knew that maintenance dosage was never given hypodermically except in cases of extreme emergency when immediate results are desired. He positively denied that Mrs. Evans showed him the ampules of injectible Lanoxin and denied seeing them although he concedes she might have had the ampules in her hand without his having seen them. He further stated he was well aware that a 3 c.c. injection of Lanoxin would be fatal to such a small child. Dr. Beskin also testifies that he was clearly of the impression Mrs. Evans was referring solely to the quantity to be administered and at no time was he led to believe she desired information about the method or routine of administration. If he had even remotely suspected that she referred to the drug in its injectible form he would have warned her. His testimony clearly shows that, because of the nature of the drug, in his opinion, the better practice is to specify the route or method of administration on the order sheet. His testimony is devoid of reference to any custom or practice to the effect that if route of administration is not specified it signifies the drug is to be given orally.

Dr. Ruiz's testimony is also somewhat in conflict with that of Mrs. Evans as to what conversation transpired between them. According to Dr. Ruiz, Mrs. Evans, standing in the doorway to the medicine room, showed him an ampule of Lanoxin and asked him about it. From Mrs. Evans' inquiry Dr. Ruiz understood that she had been ordered to administer the medication hypodermically and was of the further impression that her inquiry was whether 1 c.c of the drug given by injection was excessive. He told her that in one dose, it (he referring to "it" as a c.c. by injection) was a large dose for an infant and that it would be better for Mrs. Evans to consult the attending physician who wrote the order. According to Dr. Ruiz, he then obtained the medicine which prompted his visit to the medicine room and left. Dr. Ruiz testified positively that it is the policy for nurses to call the attending physicians when there is doubt or uncertainty about an order for medication. He also stated that in his own experience he has been called numerous times by nurses who desired explanation or clarification of his orders. Dr. Ruiz did not testify regarding the alleged custom or understanding that orders for medication are intended to be by oral route unless otherwise specified. He did testify, however, that in his opinion, the better practice is to specify both route and amount of any drug prescribed. The testimony of Dr. Ruiz makes it quite clear that in his opinion, a nurse who is unaware of the fact that Lanoxin is prepared in oral form is not properly trained and instructed for duty in a pediatric ward.

Dr. Charles N. Bombet, Pediatrician, in substance testified that in his opinion, the better practice and the procedure which he always followed was to specify the route of administration when the drug prescribed was capable of administration by multiple route. He further testified that the nature and potency of Lanoxin is such that even though he prescribes the drug rather frequently in his practice he does not trust to memory with respect to dosages but instead carries upon his person at all times a pocket sized manufacturer's chart furnished physicians. Dr. Bombet also testified that he never prescribes the drug without referring to the chart in question to determine dosage. He stated that it is his practice to always indicate in some manner the route of administration he intends. As did the other medical experts he also testified that it is the custom and practice for nurses who are in doubt regarding a physician's order to consult the physician who wrote the order.

Jimmie Dean Westbrook, a registered nurse, testified in substance that if she had read Dr. Stotler's order of January 2, 1960, to give 3 c.c. of Lanoxin today for one dose only, she does not know how she would have interpreted it at that time. She was, however, familiar with Lanoxin in its elixir form and had forgotten that she had administered the elixir to the Norton infant when the baby was first hospitalized. According to Westbrook, her policy is that when in doubt about an order for medication she calls the attending physician.

Mrs. Helen W. Sheehan, Director of Nursing Services, Baton Rouge General Hospital, testified that since the incident involving the Norton baby she has instituted a rule in the hospital that all nurses must indicate on the chart by means of a system of symbols the route of administration of all drugs and that nurses are to assume the route to be oral unless otherwise specified by the attending physician. Mrs. Sheehan is of the opinion that the better practice (which she follows) is that in case of doubt the attending physician should be contacted regarding an order for medication. She declined to testify that it was the general practice in the nursing profession to assume that where route was not specified oral administration was intended. She had been taught that oral route was intended unless otherwise specified but did not know what was taught on the subject as a general rule although she conceded that some books on Pharmacology advocated the practice of oral administration in the absence of specific orders to the contrary. To her knowledge the hospital never adopted a policy as to what course a nurse should follow in the event of doubt concerning an order for medicine. In her own case Mrs. Sheehan followed what she considered the better practice of consulting the attending physician in case of uncertainty.

Miss Shirley M. Meadows, student nurse on duty in the pediatric ward January 2, 1960, in substance corroborated the testimony of Mrs. Evans relative to the latter's conversations with Doctors Beskin and Ruiz. She denied that in her nurse's training she was taught that when route of administration was not specified oral administration of medication was intended. She likewise denied knowledge of any rule, custom or practice in the hospital to the effect that where route was not mentioned oral administration was presumed to be the route intended. According to Miss Meadows what is usually done in such instances is that the nurse relies upon her knowlege of the medicaton and experience gained from prior administration of the particular drug. She further testified that the normal procedure in instances of doubt is to call either the hospital pharmacy or the physician who prescribed the medication to be administered a patient.

Miss Barbara Jean Sipes, the registered nurse in charge of the Pediatric unit on the day in question, in essence testified that she heard nothing of the conversation between Mrs. Evans and Dr. Beskin although she did see them talking. She heard at least a portion of the discussion between Mrs. Evans and Dr. Ruiz but did not hear Dr. Ruiz advise Mrs. Evans to call the attending physician. According to Miss Sipes, Mrs. Evans discussed the problem with her and the manner in which the disputed order was written led both Miss Sipes and Mrs. Evans to believe and understand that the medication was intended to be routed intramuscularly. She stated that designation of the quantity in cubic centimeters to her meant injection. Upon her memory being refreshed from information on the child's hospital chart, she recalled having administered the infant Lanoxin orally on the baby's previous hospitalization but commented that at that time it was prescribed "Elixir" which was different from the order of January 2, 1960. Until just a few days prior to trial of this case she had never heard that oral administration was meant and intended unless otherwise specified. She was taught, considered it the best practice and followed the rule of consulting the prescribing physician when in doubt about an order for medication.

Miss Joan O. Walsh (the nurse in charge of the Pediatric Unit) testified that she was off duty on the day in question. When queried about the order in question she repeatedly testified that because of the manner in which it was written she does not know exactly how she would have interpreted it at the time. She intimated, however, that in view of her familiarity with Lanoxin and the fact that she had previously administered oral Lanoxin to the Norton child on the baby's prior admission to the hospital she might have understood the order to intend oral route. . .

From the foregoing resume of the testimony appearing in the record of this case it is manifest that Dr. Stotler was negligent in failing to denote the intended route of administration and failing to indicate that the medication prescribed had already been given or was to be given by the patient's mother. It is conceded by counsel for Dr. Stotler that the doctor's oversight in this regard exposed the child to the distinct possibility of being given a double oral dose of the medicine. Although it is by no means certain from the evidence that a second dose of oral Lanoxin would have proven fatal, Dr. Stotler's own testimony does not make it clear that in all probability it would have produced nausea. In this regard his testimony is to the effect that even if the strength of two oral doses were sufficient to produce death in all probability death would not result for the reason that nausea produced by overdosing would have most probably induced the child to vomit the second dose thereby saving her life.

The contention that Dr. Stotler followed the practice and custom usually engaged in by similar practitioners in the community is clearly refuted and contradicted by the evidence of record herein. Of the four medical experts who testified herein only Dr. Stotler testified in effect that it was the customary and usual practice to write a prescription in the manner shown. The testimony of Drs. Beskin, Bombet and Ruiz falls far short of corroborating Dr. Stotler in this important aspect. The testimony of Dr. Stotler's colleagues was clearly to the effect that the better practice is to specify the route of administration intended. Doctors Breskin and Bombet further testified that in their own practice they follow the procedure of indicating in some manner what method of administration they desire. In this connection we note the herein above mentioned testimony of Dr. Bombet to the effect that Lanoxin being such a potent and highly specialized drug, he at all times carries on his person a pocket chart provided by the manufacturer for use by physicians and always consults the chart before prescribing dosage rather than rely upon his memory. While it is conceded his testimony in this respect clearly shows that he consults the chart merely to refresh his memory as to dosage, it nevertheless indicates the importance which he attaches to the necessity of being accurate when dealing with this particular medication. In view of the foregoing, we hold that the act acknowledged by Dr. Stotler does not relieve him from liability to plaintiffs herein on the ground that it accorded with that degree of skill and care employed, under similar circumstances, by other members of his profession in good standing in the community. We find and hold that the record before us fails to establish that physicians in good standing in the community follow the procedure adopted by defendant herein but rather the contrary is shown.

. . .[I]t is the settled jurisprudence of this state that a hospital is responsible for the negligence of its employees including, inter alia, nurses and attendants under the doctrine of *respondeat superior* . . .

In the case at bar it is not disputed that Mrs. Evans was not only an employee of the hospital but that on the day in question she was in charge of the entire institution as the senior employee on duty at the time.

Although there have been instances in our jurisprudence wherein the alleged negligence of nurses has been made the basis of an action for damages for personal injuries resulting therefrom, we are not aware of any prior decision which fixes the responsibility or duty of care owed by nurses to patients under their care or treatment. The general rule, however, seems to be to extend to nurses the same rules which govern the duty and liability of physicians in the performance of professional services . . .

The foregoing rule appears to be well founded and we see no valid reason why it should not be adopted as the law of this state. Tested in the light of the rule herein above enunciated the negligence of Mrs. Evans is patent upon the face of the record. We readily agree with the statement of Dr. Ruiz that a nurse who is unfamiliar with the fact that the drug in question is prepared in oral form for administration to infants by mouth is not properly and adequately trained for duty in a pediatric ward. As laudable as her intentions are conceded to have been on the occasion in question, her unfamiliarity with the drug was a contributing factor in the child's death. In this regard we are of the opinion that she was negligent in attempting to administer a drug with which she was not familiar. While we concede that a nurse does not have the same degree of knowledge regarding drugs as is possessed by members of the medical profession, nevertheless, common sense dictates that no nurse should attempt to administer a drug under the circumstances shown in the case at bar. Not only was Mrs. Evans unfamiliar with the medicine in question but she also violated what has been shown to be the rule generally practiced by the members of the nursing profession in the community and which rule, we might add, strikes us as being most reasonable and prudent, namely, the practice of calling the prescribing physician, when in doubt about an order for medication. True, Mrs. Evans attempted to verify the order by inquiring of Doctors Beskin and Ruiz but evidently there was a complete lack of communication with these individuals. The record leaves no doubt but that neither Doctor Beskin nor Doctor Ruiz was made aware of just what Mrs. Evans intended to administer. Dr. Beskin was of the impression she referred to oral Lanoxin and Dr. Ruiz was of the impression she intended only 1 cubic centimenter of the injectible. For obvious reasons we believe it the duty of a nurse when in doubt about an order for medication to make absolutely certain what the doctor intended both as to dosage and route. In the case at bar the evidence leaves not the slightest doubt that whereas nurses in the locality do at times consult any available physician, it appears equally certain that all of the nurses who testified herein agree that the better practice (and the one which they follow) is to consult the prescribing physician when in doubt about an order for medication. With regard to nurses consulting any available physician when in doubt about an order for medication, the testimony of Drs. Beskin and Ruiz indicates clearly that in their experience such inquiries are generally restricted solely to interpretation of the doctor's handwriting and are not usually related to dosage or route. Having elected to deviate from the general and better practice of consulting the physician who ordered the medication in question, Mrs. Evans was under the duty and obligation of making herself understood beyond the possibility of error. This she did not do as has herein previously been shown. It appears reasonably clear that had she consulted Dr. Stotler and advised him of her intention to administer the 3 c.cs. of Lanoxin hypodermically he would have warned her of the danger and this tragic accident would not have occurred . . .

The evidence in the case at bar leaves not the slightest doubt that when Dr. Stotler entered the order for the medication on the chart, it was the duty of the hospital nursing staff to administer it. Dr. Stotler frankly concedes this important fact and for that reason acknowledged that he should have indicated on the chart that the medication had been given or was to be given by the mother, otherwise some nurses on the pediatric unit would give it as was required of the hospital staff. Not only was there a duty on the part of Dr. Stotler to make this clear so as to prevent duplication of the medication but also he was under the obligation of specifying or in some manner indicating the route considering the drug is prepared in two forms in which dosage is measured in cubic centimeters. In dealing with modern drugs, especially of the type with which we are herein concerned, it is the duty of the prescribing physician who knows that the prescribed medication will be administered by a nurse or third party, to make certain as to the lines of communication between himself and the party whom he knows will ultimately execute his orders. Any failure in such communication which may prove fatal or injurious to the patient must be charged to the prescribing physician who has full knowledge of the drug and its effects upon the human system. The duty of communication between physician and nurse is more important when we consider that the nurse who administers the medication is not held to the same degree of knowledge with respect thereto as the prescribing physician. It, therefore, becomes the duty of the physician to make his intentions clear and unmistakable. If, as the record shows, Dr. Stotler had ordered Elixir Lanoxin, or specified the route to be oral, it would have clearly informed all nurses of his intention to administer the medication by mouth. Instead, however, he wrote his order in an uncertain, confusing manner considering that the drug in question comes in oral and injectible form and that in both forms dosage is prescribed in terms of cubic centimeters . . .

The doctrine of independent, intervening cause invoked by defendant Aetna herein on the ground that conceding Dr. Stotler's negligence, the independent, intervening negligence of Mrs. Evans was so unforseeable and unpredictable as to render Dr. Stotler's negligence a remote rather than a proximate cause of the child's death is without foundation in the record . . .

. . . That the negligence of Dr. Stotler was a substantial factor in bringing about the death of the Norton child appears so obvious as to warrant little discussion. In this connection we believe it suffices to say that if the order had been written so that it could be clearly understood the untimely death of the child would not have resulted therefrom. Moreover, it appears from the testimony of at least two of the nurses who testified herein that prescribing the drug in cubic centimeters indicated to them that it was to be administered by intramuscular injection. We believe it safe to say that except for the manner in which the prescription was written, the accident would not have occurred.

Moreover, however, what appears to us to be the more logical conclusion is that the negligence of Aetna's insured foreseeably produced the death of plaintiff's child. We believe the testimony of Doctors Bombet and Beskin make it clear that the better practice is to specify the route of administration to avoid the possibility of error in dealing with a drug of the nature and character with which we are herein concerned. Failure to specify the route of a drug which, measured in c.cs. may be administered either orally or by injection is, in our view, calculated to produce confusion and uncertainty which may foreseeably result in the drug being administered in either form one of which may prove fatal. Misinterpretation of the order as written being foreseeable under the circumstances, such misconstruction cannot serve as the basis of rendering the physician's negligence remote rather than proximate. Rather than being incomprehensible and inconceivable as defendant Aetna contends, it appears such misconstruction is foreseeable and likely under the circumstances shown in the case at bar . . .

Amended and affirmed.

o **Recap of the Case.** This case illustrates two of the most common types of nursing malpractice: improper exercise of nursing skills and administration of an improper medication or solution. Major factors contributing to this particular instance of negligence were continued administration of medication by the patient's mother while the patient was in the hospital, failure of the nurse involved to recognize that her nursing skills were no longer current, and the entry by the attending physician of a confusing medication order in the patient's chart which the nurse failed to clarify. All of these contributing factors can be avoided. The practical lesson of this case is that avoidance of these factors will contribute to the avoidance of nursing liability.

NURSES AND HOSPITAL LIABLE FOR FAILURE TO OBSERVE PATIENT PROPERLY

Nurses have a duty to observe their patients and to report their observations appropriately. In *Darling v. Charleston Community Memorial Hospital*, 33 Ill.2d 326, 211 N.E.2d 253 (1965), nurses and the hospital were found liable for failure to properly observe the patient's leg following placement of a cast on the leg. The leg subsequently became gangrenous and had to be amputated.

Darling v. Charleston Community Memorial Hospital
33 Ill.2d 326, 211 N.E.2d 253 (1965) Supreme Court of Illinois

. . . On November 5, 1960, the plaintiff, who was 18 years old, broke his leg while playing in a college football game. He was taken to the emergency room at the defendant hospital where Dr. Alexander, who was on emergency call that day, treated him. Dr. Alexander, with the assistance of hospital personnel applied traction and placed the leg in a plaster cast. A heat cradle was applied to dry the cast. Not long after the application of the cast plaintiff was in great pain and his toes, which protruded from the cast, became swollen and dark in color. They eventually became cold and insensitive. On the evening of November 6, Dr. Alexander "notched" the cast around the toes, and on the afternoon of the next day he cut the cast approximately three inches up from the foot. On Novermber 8 he split the sides of the cast with a Stryker saw; in the course of cutting the cast the plaintiff's leg was cut on both sides. Blood and other seepage were observed by the nurses and others, and there was a stench in the room, which one witness said was the worst he had smelled since World War II. The plaintiff remained in Charleston Hospital until November 19, when he was transferred to Barnes Hospital in St. Louis and placed under the care of Dr. Fred Reynolds, head of orthopedic surgery at Washington University School of Medicine and Barnes Hospital. Dr. Reynolds found that the fractured leg contained a considerable amount of dead tissue which in his opinion resulted from interference with the circulation of blood in the limb caused by swelling or hemorrhaging of the leg against the construction of the cast. Dr. Reynolds performed several operations in a futile attempt to save the leg but ultimately it had to be amputated eight inches below the knee.

The evidence before the injury is set forth at length in the opinion of the Appellate Court and need not be stated in detail here. The plaintiff contends that it established that the defendant was negligent in permitting Dr. Alexander to do orthopedic work of the kind required in this case, and not requiring him to review his operative procedures to bring them up to date; in failing, through its medical staff, to exercise adequate supervision over the case, especially since Dr. Alexander had been placed on emergency duty by the hospital, and in not requiring consultation, particularly after complications had developed. Plaintiff contends also that in a case which developed as this one did, it was the duty of the nurses to watch the protruding toes constantly for changes of color, temperature and movement, and to check circulation every ten to twenty minutes, whereas the proof showed that these things were done only a few times a day. Plaintiff argues that it was the duty of the hospital staff to see that these procedures were followed, and that either the nurses were derelict in failing to report developments in the case to the hospital administrator, he was derelict in bringing them to the attention of the medical staff, or the staff was negligent in failing to take action. Defendant is a licensed and accredited hospital, and the plaintiff contends that the licensing regulations, accreditation standards, and its own bylaws define the hospital's duty, and that an infraction of them imposes liability for the resulting injury.

The defendant's position is stated in the following excerpts from its brief: "It is a fundamental rule of law that only an individual properly educated and licensed, and not a corporation, may practice medicine . . . Accordingly, a hospital is powerless under the law to forbid or command any act by a physician or surgeon in the practice of his profession . . . A hospital is not an insurer of the patient's recovery, but only owes the patient the duty to exercise such reasonable care as his known condition requires and that degree of care, skill and diligence used by hospitals generally in that community . . . Where the evidence shows that the hospital care was in accordance with standard practice obtaining in similar hospitals, and Plaintiff produces no evidence to the contrary, the jury cannot conclude that the opposite is true even if they disbelieve the hospital witnesses . . . A hospital is not liable for the torts of its nurse committed while the nurse was but executing the orders of the patient's physician, unless such order is so obviously negligent as to lead any reasonable person to anticipate that substantial injury would result to the patient from the execution of such order . . . The extent of the duty of a hospital with respect to actual medical care of a professional nature such as is furnished by a physician is to use reasonable care in selecting medical doctors. When such care in the selection of the staff is accomplished, and nothing indicates that a physician so selected is incompetent or that such incompetence should have been discovered, more cannot be expected from the hospital administration." . . .

As has been seen, the defendant argues in this court that its duty is to be determined by the care customarily offered by hospitals generally in its community. Strictly speaking, the question is not one of duty, for " . . . in negligence cases, the duty is always the same, to conform to the legal standards of reasonable conduct in the light of the apparent risk. What the defendant must do, or must not do, is a question of the standard of conduct required to satisfy the duty" . . . "By the great weight of modern American authority a custom either to take or to omit a precaution is generally admissable as bearing on what is proper conduct under the circumstances, but is not conclusive" . . . Custom is relevant in determining the standard of care because it illustrates what is feasible, it suggests a body of knowledge of which the defendant should be aware, and it warns of the possibility of far-reaching consequences if a higher standard is required . . . But custom should never be conclusive . . .

In the present case the regulations, standards, and bylaws which the plaintiff introduced into evidence, performed much the same function as did evidence of custom. This evidence aided the jury in deciding what was feasible and what the defendant knew or should have known. It did not conclusively determine the standard of care and the jury was not instructed that it did.

"The conception that the hospital does not undertake to treat the patient, does not undertake to act through its doctors and nurses, but undertakes instead simply to procure them to act upon their own responsibility, no longer reflects the fact. Present-day hospitals, as their manner of operation plainly demonstrates, do far more than furnish facilities for treatment. They regularly employ on a salary basis a large staff of physicians, nurses and internes, as well as administrative and manual workers, and they charge patients for medical care and treatment, collecting for such services, if necessary, by legal action. Certainly, the person who avails himself of 'hospital facilities' expects that the hospital will attempt to cure him, not that its nurses or other employees will act on their own responsibility." . . . The Standards for Hospital Accreditation, the state licensing regulations and the defendant's bylaws demonstrate that the medical profession and other responsible authorities regard it as both desirable and feasible that a hospital assume certain responsibilities for the care of the patient . . . Two of [these issues] were that the defendant had negligently:

"Failed to have a sufficient number of trained nurses . . . for bedside care of all patients at all times capable of recognizing the progressive gangrenous condition of the plaintiff's right leg, and of bringing the same to the attention of the hospital administration and to the medical staff so that adequate consultation could have been secured and such conditions rectified . . . Failed to require consultation with or examination by members of the hospital surgical staff skilled in such treatment; or to review the treatment rendered to the plaintiff and to require consultants to be called in as needed."

We believe that the jury verdict is supportable on either of these grounds. On the basis of the evidence before it the jury could reasonably have concluded that the nurses did not test for circulation in the leg as frequently as necessary, that skilled nurses would have promptly recognized the conditions that signalled a dangerous impairment of circulation in the plaintiff's leg, and would have known that the condition would become irreversible in a matter of hours. At that point it became the nurses' duty to inform the attending physician, and if he failed to act, to advise the hospital authorities so that appropriate action might be taken. As to consultation, there is no dispute that the hospital failed to review Dr. Alexander's work or require a consultation; the only issue is whether its failure to do so was negligence. On the evidence before it the jury could reasonably have found that it was . . .

The judgment of the Appellate Court for the Fourth District is affirmed.

o **Recap of the Case.** The patient presented evidence which showed that the failure of nurses to properly observe the condition of his broken leg and to report signs of gangrene to the proper personnel resulted in the amputation of his leg. The court determined that the hospital had an obligation to provide adequate nursing staff to carry out this function. Because the hospital did not provide adequate staff as required, it too was responsible for the patient's injuries.

FAILURE TO FOLLOW PROPER PROCEDURES RESULTS IN LIABILITY FOR PATIENT'S FALL

Falls frequently result in liability for nurses. In *Burks v. Christ Hospital*, 19 Ohio St.2d 128, 249, N.E.2d 829 (1969), for example, an obese patient in severe pain who was sedated to the point of disorientation was placed in a bed with no side rails. It should come as no surprise that she fell out of bed.

It should be noted that the court was extremely critical of the hospital because it lacked a nursing procedures manual. Such a manual should have been available to the nurses involved in this incident so that the proper precautions to be taken under the circumstances were clear. An important nursing function is delineation of the proper standard of care. Nurses, regardless of practice setting, should work to develop these standards for the benefit of the patient and to assist nurses to avoid liability for falls.

Burks v. Christ Hospital,
19 Ohio St.2d 128, 249 N.E.2d 829 (1969).
Supreme Court of Ohio

. . . According to Dr. Lloyd Larrick, the administrator of the The Christ Hospital, the hospital did not have a service operation manual for nursing personnel in May of 1960 when plaintiff's injuries occurred.

In The Christ Hospital School of Nursing, which is a training school for nurses under the control of the same board of directors as The Christ Hospital, there was in use a "Nurses' Procedures Manual," which sets forth the rules that were taught to the nurses as good operating rules for the normal standard of care to be followed by a nurse in caring for a patient in the hospital.

This manual provided that side rails should always be applied to the bed of a patient who is restless, very obese, under deep sedation, or in any other case where side rails would be an added protection, and provided further that any omission of side rails, when the patient's condition would seem to warrant it, must be on written order of the attending physician. The manual also provided that if the patient is permitted to get up alone, or if he is likely to get up without permission, the rollers on the bed must be removed rather than apply side rails.

Dr. Larrick testified that the teaching manual prescribed a standard of care which the nurses who graduate from the School of Nursing are to follow in the care of patients, whether they work at The Christ Hospital or any other hospital. There is evidence in the record that other hospitals in the Cincinnati community used as their operating standards for care of patients the standards of care set forth in this nursing school teaching manual.

In the instant case, plaintiff was placed in a bed which had rollers and raised side rails on it the first day that she was in the hospital. She was then transferred to a bed which had rollers, but no side rails, and it was from this bed that she fell. The evidence showed that she had been given drugs during the four days prior to the time she fell from her bed and that she was in a sedated, foggy and disoriented state at the time she fell. On the day before she fell, she was allowed to get up once to go to the bathroom, but because she was so short of stature and obese she was provided with a footstool to help her get from and to her bed, at which time she was assisted by a nurses' aid. The patient's doctor testified for the defense that he had not ordered side rails because he wanted the patient to be up and around.

Where a short, obese hospital patient, who is in severe pain, is placed in a hospital bed with rollers and without side rails and sedated to the point where she is foggy, drowsy and disoriented, and while under the effects of this sedation she falls from her bed and is injured, it is a jury question as to whether the hospital was negligent in not applying raised side rails to the bed, and, if the jury finds that the hospital was negligent, it is then a question for the jury to determine whether that negligence was the proximate cause of the injury which the patient suffered . . .

Under such circumstances, expert opinion is not controlling as to what the rules, regulations, customs or standards of care are with regard to the application of side rails to a bed in a hospital. In considering the question of the negligence of the hospital, the jury must determine whether the hospital exercised reasonable care in promulgating and enforcing rules to protect the patient against the dangers incident to the patient's condition . . .

With regard to the question of proximate cause, the Court of Appeals was in error in its conclusion that "no one knows just how she got from the bed to the floor." The defendant, in its answer, admitted that the plaintiff fell from the bed to the floor at the time she alleged in her petition.

The judgment of the Court of Appeals is, therefore, reversed and the judgment of the trial court affirmed.

o **Recap of the Case.** In order to establish negligence, the plaintiff must first establish the standard of care. Patients routinely use nursing policies and procedures to determine the standard. However, in this case, the hospital had no written procedures to follow for the prevention of falls. The court then determined what the standard was and that it was in fact breached. The practical point to be made is that nurses can control to a large extent what the standard of practice is through the development of comprehensive policies and procedures. When expectations are clearly outlined, nurses are assisted to avoid liability.

NURSES NOT RESPONSIBLE FOR PATIENT'S FALL

The "good news" concerning falls is that sometimes patients fall, and nurses are not liable. A decision is made that the nursing staff exercised proper care, but the patient fell anyway. *Killgore v. Argonaut–Southwest Insurance Company*, 216 So.2d 108 (La.App. 1968) is an example of such a case.

The patient in this case was alert and able to call a nurse for assistance. She was placed in a bed, and the guard rails were placed in the upright position. The patient fell when she apparently attempted to climb over the rails to get out of bed. The plaintiff sued, claiming that the nursing staff had a responsibility to watch the patient continuously. The court rejected the plaintiff's claim. According to the court, the nursing staff at a hospital is not responsible to provide continuous care. If such care is required, it is the patient's responsibility to employ additional nurses to provide this level of care.

Killgore v. Argonaut–Southwest Insurance Company
216 So.2d 108 (La.App. 1968) Louisiana Court of Appeals

For cause of action the plaintiffs allege negligence on the part of the hospital in failing to require someone to look out for the safety of Mrs. Cora Killgore on a continuous basis; and in failing to provide adequate guard rails on the side of the bed occupied by Mrs. Killgore. In the assignment of written reasons by the trial judge he found the hospital was negligent on both counts.

Mrs. Cora Killgore was admitted to the Homer Memorial Hospital on October 8, 1965 at the request of her treating physician, Dr. Grover C. Black, Jr., of Homer for treatment of acute pleurisy and pneumonia. At the time the patient was 88 years of age, was not ambulatory, and had been confined to a wheel chair for several months. She became a ward patient in the hospital and occupied a room with one or more other patients.

During the early morning hours of October 12, Audrey Johnson and Mary E. Mason, two nurses on duty at the hospital heard the sound of a fall and an outcry from Mrs. Killgore and immediately went to her room where they found her lying on the floor beside her bed. Shortly before this occurred both nurses had checked the patient and had observed that she was sleeping. Although Mrs. Ruby Killgore had spent a considerable number of hours at the bedside of Mrs. Killgore, no member of the family was present at the time of the fall. As a result of falling to the floor the patient sustained a fracture of the right hip for which surgical correction was required. After recovery from her original illness and from the surgery for the hip fracture Mrs. Killgore returned to the home of her sons where she resided until her death on February 13, 1966, her death being caused by conditions not related to her fall.

Mrs. Killgore, despite her age, was described by the hospital attendants, Dr. Black, and members of her own family as an alert and understanding person. She was fully capable of using the signal device on her bed to summon a nurse to attend to her needs. As hereinafter shown by the evidence, at the time she fell from her bed it was equipped with full length side rails which were raised in an up position. She afterwards told Mrs. Johnson that she attempted to climb over the bed rail. Although some of the plaintiffs testified they informed the nursing supervisor, Claudia Miller, their mother had a bad habit of rolling out of bed, none requested that extra nurses or sitters be engaged. As we understand the testimony of Dr. Black, he could not definitely remember making a request that someone be in constant attendance at the bedside; but that he usually discussed such matters with the family and the nursing staff. Upon her admission and thereafter Mrs. Killgore was in fact attended a greater portion of the time by her daughter-in-law, Mrs. Ruby Killgore. At other times she was visited by members of the family. However, when she fell no one was in attendance.

The evidence discloses there was no clear directive to the hospital from the patient or a member of her family or from Dr. Black, her attending physician, that there be an attendant at all times. The record reveals that when extra nurses' aids (sitters) are required for a hospital patient the engagement of such extra services is a contractual obligation of the patient, or of relatives or friends. The practice at the Homer Hospital and other hospitals in the area will only be provided through a special agreement to that effect. It is customary for the hospitals located in the same area to suggest the names of available sitters and not to provide a member of their own staff.

A private hospital is not an insurer of a patient's safety . . .

Our conclusion is that there was no breach of duty by the hospital in failing to require someone to look out for the safety of Mrs. Cora Killgore on a continuous basis.

Plaintiffs have entirely failed to substantiate their allegations that the hospital was negligent in failing to provide adequate guard rails on the side of the bed occupied by Mrs. Killgore. The great weight of evidence is to this effect and supported by the testimony of Audrey Johnson, Mary Mason, Claudia Miller, Evelyn Baker, Gloria Maddry and Felton Alexander, the maintenance engineer.

For the reasons hereinabove set forth, the judgment appealed from is annulled and set aside and the demands of plaintiffs are rejected at their cost.

Reversed.

o Recap of the Case. In this case, the nursing staff took proper precautions to prevent the patient from falling from her bed. The guard rails were up on the bed, and the call button was convenient for the patient to reach. The patient, who was alert, apparently attempted to climb over the rails and fell. She argued that the standard of care required that the nursing staff watch her continuously. The court rejected this standard and determined that the nurses had fulfilled their duty to this patient.

6

Defenses

Needless to say, not every claim for negligence is successful. There are defenses to plaintiffs' negligence claims which defendant practitioners utilize to preclude liability. These defenses include: 1) assumption of the risk; 2) contributory negligence; 3) tolling of the statute of limitations; 4) releases and waivers; and 5) counter-suits.

In order to claim assumption of the risk as a defense to negligence, the defendant must prove that the plaintiff gave consent in advance to relieve the defendant of a duty toward the plaintiff and to take the chances of injury from a known risk arising from what the defendant is to do or leave undone. In order to prove this defense, the defendant must show that: 1) the plaintiff knew and understood the risk incurred; and 2) the plaintiff's choice to incur the risk was entirely free and voluntary.

PHYSICIAN NOT LIABLE FOR PATIENT'S DEATH FOLLOWING ARTIFICIAL HEART IMPLANTATION

Assumption of the risk is a complete defense to a claim of negligence; if the defendant can prove assumption of the risk, he is not held liable. The defense of assumption of the risk is often used in cases involving experimental treatment. In *Karp v. Cooley*, 349 F.Supp. 827 (S.D.Tex. 1972), for example, Dr. Denton Cooley was not liable for the death of a patient following the implantation of an experimental artificial heart because the patient had voluntarily agreed to take the risk of surgery with full knowledge of the dangers involved.

Karp, the patient in this case, had a long history of heart disease. It eventually became apparent that the only thing that would save his life was a heart transplant. Because no heart was immediately available, his physician, Dr. Cooley, discussed with Karp the possibility of temporary use of a mechanical heart. The mechanical heart would be replaced with a transplant as soon as possible. Cooley discussed the use of the mechanical heart with Karp several times, and then asked him to sign a special consent form regarding the mechanical heart. This form clearly stated that the mechanical device was experimental and had never been used in humans before.

Karp's condition gradually deteriorated to the point of death. Still no heart was available. Cooley operated and inserted the mechanical device, which functioned properly and kept Karp alive until a transplant was available. The transplant was performed successfully, but Karp died shortly thereafter.

Mrs. Karp then sued Cooley for negligence. One of Cooley's defenses was that Karp assumed the risk. He knew and understood the risk as evidenced by the consent form, and his decision to undergo this experimental procedure was entirely free and voluntary. The court affirmed Cooley's argument, and he was not held liable.

Karp v. Cooley, 349 F. Supp. 827 (S.D.Tex. 1972)
United States District Court

. . . Haskell Karp had a medical history revealing past coronary problems. He had scarlet fever at the age of fifteen. In 1959, at the age of thirty-seven, he had his first heart attack and was hospitalized approximately two months because of diffuse anterior myocardial infarction. In 1961, he began to have episodes of ventricular extrasystoles and was placed on Quinidine. In 1963, he suffered another episode of severe chest pains. In 1966, he has a second acute myocardial infarction on the diaphragmatic surface. After 1966, Mr. Karp had four or five other episodes of infarction or possibly coronary insufficiency. Several times he was hospitalized with severe chest pains but with no EKG or enzyme changes. In April, 1968, he had a syncopal episode and subsequently had an implantation of a Demand pacemaker (heart pacer) placed transvenously into the right ventricle. In September, 1968, he had begun to have episodes of dyspnea, orthopnea, paroxysmal nocturnal dyspnea and developed congestive heart failure. Because of this his pacemaker rate was increased to 72 beats per minute. In spite of this action, he developed heart failure, complained of angina, dyspnea on exertion and edema. Selective cine coronary arteriograms revealed that he had severe three vessel disease, occluded right coronary and also his anterior descending and circumflex branches were occluded somewhat distally. Cardiac catheterization confirmed the fact that he had moderate pulmonary hypertension. A left ventricular cine angiogram showed the presence of an adynamic area in the left lateral wall of the left ventricle. At this point in Mr. Karp's medical history, his Chicago, Illinois, physicians referred him to Dr. Denton Cooley in Houston, Texas, for further treatment and consideration of resection of the adynamic or fibrotic area of the myocardium.

Accordingly, on Monday, March 3, 1969, Mrs. Karp telephoned Dr. Cooley long–distance to set a day when he might see Mr. Karp. Two days later, Wednesday, March 3, 1969, Haskell Karp, 47, accompanied by his wife, was admitted to St. Luke's Episcopal Hospital, Houston, Texas. Upon admission, Mr. Karp signed (as was later established at trial by a handwriting expert) an authorization for medical and/or surgical treatment (TR. EX. 1) which reads:

> I hereby authorize the physician or physicians in charge of Haskell (None) Karp to administer any treatment; or to administer such anesthetics; and perform such operations as may be deemed necessary or advisable in the diagnosis and treatment of this patient.
>
> Date: 3/5/69
> Signed: /s/ Haskell Karp
>
> Witness: /s/ Wauneta F. Tappan

Mr. Karp remained as a patient in the hospital for several weeks being examined and treated by several doctors associated with the hospital. During this period of time, Dr. Cooley suggested that Mr. Karp's desire for a more active and productive life–style could best be achieved by a heart transplant. Mr. Karp rejected this suggestion and preferred to undergo ventriculoplasty surgery (wedge procedure) which Dr. Cooley had developed . . . This surgery necessitates the excision of part of the diseased tissues in the left ventricle in order that the remaining tissue and heart muscle can function at its optimal level.

As regards the informed consent issue, Dr. Cooley testified that he discussed various aspects of the surgery in question with Mr. Karp on at least three occasions: once the week before April 4, again at 10:30 p.m. on the night of April 2, and a brief chat on April 3. According to Dr. Cooley's testimony, of these the most significant was that of April 2. On that occasion, Dr. Cooley explained to Mr. Karp that the ventriculoplasty surgery could be performed on Friday, April 4, 1969. Dr. Cooley testified he explained the risks, grave dangers and backup procedures involved therein. Further, he explained to Mr. Karp that there was a "70–30" chance of his surviving the ventriculoplasty operation. Dr. Cooley explained, as was stated in the written consent form, that if death appeared imminent that his heart would be removed and a mechanical heart substitute (sometimes referred to as the Cooley–Liotta mechanical heart) inserted. Dr. Cooley testified that he told Mr. Karp the mechanical heart substitute would not be permanent but would be replaced as soon as possible by a human heart transplant, but that at that time there was no heart donor available, nor any prospect of one. Dr. Cooley also testified that he promised Mr. Karp he would do all that is humanly possible to insure his well–being and improve his patient's, that is, Mr. Karp's, condition. At that time, Mr. Karp gave him his verbal consent to the surgery.

Mrs. Karp testified that if Dr. Cooley did see her husband that evening (April 2, 1969) that it would have to have been very late for she usually stayed until after 10:00 p.m. with her husband. However, she also testified that on the night in question she went out to dinner at a friend's home late in the evening and did not return to the hospital that night until after this dinner and visit.

Rabbi Wilkin, a Jewish chaplain for the medical center who had been calling on Mr. Karp daily since his admission to the hospital, testified that on one of the days during the week of the surgery (week beginning Monday, March 31, 1969) Mr. Karp had an urgent message sent to him to come to his room. The Rabbi went to his room where he found Mr. Karp alone. Mr. Karp related to the Rabbi the news that he was to be operated on and discussed with the Rabbi the chances of surviving such surgery as well as the back–up procedures and the fact that he would be the first human recipient of the mechanical heart substitute if the wedge procedure failed. There was no testimony given at the trial to refute Rabbi Wilkin's statements as to his conversations with Mr. Karp.

Mrs. Karp testified that the first time she heard about the impending surgery that had been scheduled was from her husband on Thursday morning, April 3. She also stated that Dr. Cooley came to her husband's room Thursday evening and told both of them that Mr. Karp's condition had taken a turn for the worse and if surgery was not done soon Mr. Karp would die of a "burst aneurysm." Mrs. Karp felt that Dr. Cooley was insistent and very impatient for Mr. Karp to sign the specially prepared surgical consent and to be on his way. She further testified that she did not fully understand the risks involved in the various procedures; however, she did remember specifically asking Dr. Cooley what the words "mechanical cardiac substitute" meant and receiving an explanation.

Dr. Cooley testified that neither good medical standards nor his own personal practice would permit him to tell a patient that his condition was without hope and that he was going to die. Dr. Cooley also stated that his medical opinion, as repeatedly expressed in articles published prior to and subsequent to Mr. Karp's surgery, is that an aneurysm does not burst. He emphatically testified that he could not have stated to the Karps that if surgery was not done soon Mr. Karp would die of a "burst aneurysm."

In regard to Mr. Karp's condition during that first week of April, Dr. Cooley stated that he had determined that Mr. Karp's heart pacer was failing and that, if it began to skip four or five impulses a minute instead of the two or three that it was skipping, Mr. Karp's death would result. This is why the surgery was scheduled with Mr. Karp's consent two days in advance of its actual occurrence.

Mr. Henry C. Reinhard, a St. Luke's Hospital administrator, testified that Thursday, April 3, 1969, he went to Mr. Karp's room where he found Mr. Karp alone and asked him if he had any questions regarding the surgical consent. They chatted for awhile and then Mr. Reinhard left the room. Mr. Reinhard further testified that on the day of surgery, Friday, April 4, 1969, he went to Mr. Karp's room where he found both Mr. Karp and Mrs. Karp present. He asked Mr. Karp if the signature on the following consent form as principal was his true signature wherein Mr. Karp replied affirmatively. Mr. Reinhard then asked Mrs. Karp if the signature as witness on the following consent form was her true signature wherein she replied affirmatively. Having explained to them that he wanted to verify the signature so that he could place his own name of the form, Mr. Reinhard witnessed, as Mrs. Karp had previously done, the following consent form:

I, Haskell Karp, request and authorize Dr. Denton A. Cooley and such other surgeons as he may designate to perform upon me, in St. Luke's Episcopal Hospital of Houston, Texas, cardiac surgery for advanced cardiac decompensation and myocardial insufficiency as a result of numerous coronary occlusions. The risk of this surgery has been explained to me. In the event cardiac function cannot be restored by excision of destroyed heart muscle and plastic reconstruction of the ventricle and death seems imminent, I authorize Dr. Cooley and his staff to remove my diseased heart and insert a mechanical cardiac substitute. I understand that this mechanical device will not be permanent and ultimately will require replacement by a heart transplant. I realize that this device has been tested in the laboratory but has not been used to sustain a human being and that no assurance of success can be made. I expect the surgeons to exercise every effort to preserve my life through any of these means. No assurance has been made by anyone as to the results that may be obtained.

I understand that the operating surgeon will be occupied solely with the surgery and that the administration of the anesthetic(s) is an independent function. I hereby request and authorize Dr. Arthur S. Keats, or others he may designate, to administer such anesthetics as he or they may deem advisable.

I hereby consent to the photographing of the operation to be performed, including appropriate portions of my body, for medical, scientific, and educational purposes.

WITNESSES: */Signature/s/Haskell Karp*
                                     HASKELL KARP

/s/Mrs. Haskell Karp
Mrs. Haskell Karp (wife)

/s/Henry C. Reinhard, Jr.
Henry C. Reinhard, Jr.

In the early afternoon of April 4, 1969, Mr. Karp was rolled into the hall of the surgical ward. Dr. Arthur S. Keats, the anesthesiologist, passed the patient on his way to the operating room at approximately 1:55 p.m. Dr. Keats testified that he was alarmed by Mr. Karp's groaning and complaints of shortness of breath. Dr. Keats further testified that after observing Mr. Karp's coloring and profuse sweating it was his medical opinion that Mr. Karp would expire in the hallway if something was not done immediately. Dr. Keats sent word to Dr. Cooley that the operation should begin as soon as possible, and by approximately 1:20 p.m., Mr. Karp was on the heart–lung oxgenator (commonly referred to as the heart–lung bypass machine). This procedure normally takes twice as long to complete, but the doctors testified that the procedures were hurried in an attempt to save Mr. Karp's life.

Dr. Cooley then performed the wedge procedure on Mr. Karp's left ventricle. This surgery revealed that Mr. Karp's heart had extensive scarring and damage. Approximately 35% of the left ventricle was removed. After the surgery had been completed in its normal and customary fashion, the heart began to fibrillate. This was corrected by electrocally shocking the heart. However, according to the only medical testimony given on the subject, the strength of the heart's contractions were not sufficient to sustain life in Mr. Karp. Therefore, according to back–up procedures outlined in the written consent form, Dr. Cooley, assisted by Dr. Liotta, removed the heart and implanted the mechanical heart substitute.

Mr. Karp regained consciousness and lived on the mechanical heart substitute for approximately 64 hours. During this period of time Dr. Cooley and Mrs. Karp made public appeals through the news media for a human heart donor. On April 7, 1969, at 6:30 a.m., Mr. Karp underwent surgery to remove the mechanical heart and to replace it with a human heart. His urine output was low after the first surgery, and after the second, he became anuric despite all measures to reverse the condition. Mr. Karp died on April 8, 1969, at 3:15 p.m.

An autopsy was performed revealing acute bronchopneumonia, primarily in the right lung due to pseudomonas aeruginosa, and there was evidence of tubular necrosis of the kidney with focal fibrin thrombi of the glomeruli. There was evidence of chronic passive congestion of the liver. There was evidence of hemmorragic cystitis and terminal gastric hemorrhage. There was splenomegaly with lymphoid depletion and also lymphoid depletion of the lymph nodes. His death was attributed to bronchopneumonia and acute renal failure. (Plaintiff's Exhibit No. 1)

After Mr. Karp's death, Mrs. Karp returned to her home in Illinois where she wrote numerous laudatory letters about Dr. Cooley and also wrote an outline for a book about her husband's medical experiences. This manuscript told of Mr. Karp's rapidly deteriorating physical condition before surgery and of both Mr. and Mrs. Karp's eagerness for Dr. Cooley to perform surgery on Mr. Karp. Then in the fall of 1969, Mrs. Karp individually and as Executor of the Estate of Haskell Karp, and their three sons filed suit against Doctors Cooley and Liotta for damages sustained by Mr. Karp and by plaintiffs under the Texas Wrongful Death Statute. Plaintiffs allege among other things: that the consent to the operation was fraudulently obtained; that it was not an "informed consent"; that under the circumstances the defendants were negligent in performing the corrective surgery, implanting the mechanical heart, and submitting the patient to the surgery for inserting the human donor heart; and that by fraudulent deceptive practices Mrs. Karp was used by defendants to secure a human heart donor . . .

In regard to the issue of informed consent, the Texas courts have clearly established the amount of information a doctor needs to impart to a candidate for surgery . . .

As a generalization, it may be said that every normal human being of adult years has a right to determine what shall be done to his own body, and a patient's consent is thus a necessary prerequisite to any treatment or operation. And to that may be added that one who gives his consent must have such information regarding the consequences as is necessary to form the basis of an intelligent consent. The duty of the physician to furnish the patient with sufficient information to make an intelligent decision—to disclose risks inherent in proposed treatment or surgery—is recognized . . . . One writer has observed that the reported cases present much confusion as to what risks a physician should disclose to his patient before obtaining consent to operate . . .

We have reexamined this question and have concluded that the question of what disclosure of risks incident to proposed treatment should be made in a particular situation involves medical judgment and that expert testimony thereon should be required in malpractice cases involving that issue. The question to be determined by the jury is whether defendant doctor in that particular situation failed to adhere to a standard of reasonable care. These are not matters of common knowledge or within the experience of laymen. Expert medical evidence thereon is just as necessary as is such testimony on the correctness of the handling in cases involving surgery or treatment . . . The question is not what, regarding the risks involved, the juror would relate to the patient under the same or similar circumstances, or even what a reasonable *man* would relate, but what a reasonable *medical practitioner* would do. Such practitioner would consider the state of the patient's health, the condition of his heart and nervous system, his mental state, and would take into account, among other things, whether the risks involved were mere remote possibilities or something which occurred with some sort of frequency or regularity. This determination involves medical judgment as to whether disclosure of possible risks may have such an adverse effect on the patient as to jeopardize success of the proposed therapy, no matter how expertly performed . . .

The only testimony presented by doctors from this community in the same or similar school, on the information given to patients about their surgeries in this community did not vary from the criteria just discussed, namely, that each doctor must use his medical judgment as to whether certain disclosures of risks would have an adverse effect on the patient so as to jeopardize the success of the proposed therapy. Dr. Beasley, Dr. Hamaker, Dr. Keats, and Dr. Cooley all testified that it often is advisable to deliberately withhold information from a patient that would unduly distress him. Dr. H. L. Beasley testified that this notation on Mr. Karp's chart on March 7, 1969, "I am not completely sold that this is a candidate for surgery" (Plaintiff's Exhibit No. 1--Dr. Beasley's handwritten notation of 3-7-69) had reference to Mr. Karp's poor emotional attitude toward his hospitalization. All the medical testimony stated that emotional attitude and depression would affect what they would relate to a patient.

In making the determination of what to tell a patient about his surgery, a doctor must decide on what details he will give. The courts have developed the following approach with regard to details of surgery:

Surgical operation may consist of many steps and involve many specialists. It would, indeed, be unreasonable and undesirable to place a burden of full and complete disclosure upon each and every specialist involved as to the specific methods intended to be used in an operation and all of the possible risks involved in each step of an operation . . .

Upon a review of all the evidence produced, it could not be concluded by a jury that Dr. Cooley had violated the medical standard in this community by the information he gave or did not give to Mr. Karp concerning his surgery . . .

It must also be considered at this point that the specially prepared consent form did relate some of the detailed information that plaintiffs complain of, i.e., "I realize that this device has been tested in the laboratory but has not been used to sustain a human being and that no assurance of success can be made." Texas law would require that a jury be instructed that Mr. Karp is charged with reading the consent even if in fact he did not . . .

Under Texas law the jury would also have to have been instructed that Mrs. Karp's consent to the surgery was not required. Indeed, Mrs. Karp could not legally grant consent to surgery to be performed on her husband and, therefore, any information given to her or withheld from her could not have affected the informed consent of her husband . . .

Accordingly, as to any issue of informed consent, a verdict must be directed for Dr. Cooley. Because there is no duty upon a surgeon assisting the patient's chief surgeon to acquire a separate consent form and because the two consent forms signed by Mr. Karp cover Dr. Liotta, also, defendant Liotta would likewise have to receive a directed verdict in his favor.

With regard to the issue of negligence in Texas malpractice cases, the plaintiff has the burden of establishing such negligence by the use of expert medical testimony . . .

In establishing standards of medical criteria through expert testimony, the medical articles plaintiff introduced cannot be evidence of negligence or proximate cause.

> When a doctor testifies as an expert relative to injuries or diseases he may be asked to identify a given work as a standard authority on the subject involved; and if he so recognizes it, excerpts therefrom may be read not as original evidence but solely to discredit his testimony or to test its weight . . .

Plaintiff's counsel consistently argued at trial that one article by Dr. Cooley stated that aneurysms can burst and, therefore, this contradicted Dr. Cooley's testimony that he would never tell a patient his aneurysm would burst. Plaintiff argues that this would lend some weight to the jury deciding that the defendant had misinformed Mr. Karp or that he was negligent in diagnosing and treating Mr. Karp. Dr. Cooley repeatedly testified that the articles referred to were not articles dealing with the same type of heart condition Mr. Karp suffered from and that the "burst aneurysm" account is credited to another doctor's statement not his [i.e., Dr. Cooley].

No medical expert opinion was given at trial to even suggest that Dr. Cooley or Dr. Liotta was negligent in any way in their diagnosis or surgical technique and that any such alleged negligence was the proximate cause of death. The Texas definition of negligence is failure to use ordinary care, which is use of that degree of care that medical doctors of ordinary knowledge and skill of the same school of practice of this or a similar community would use in the diagnosis, treatment, and surgery of patients under same or similar circumstances . . .

Plaintiffs subpoenaed Dr. Michael DeBakey to testify. Defense counsel argued to the court that the previously publicized alleged friction between this witness and Dr. Cooley would be highly inflammatory and serve no purpose except to introduce issues into the case before the jury that were not properly before the court. Counsel took this position because Dr. DeBakey had indicated at his deposition that he would not give any medical opinion on the Karp case or willingly answer any hypothetical question developed from the Karp case facts. In order to have expert evidence admitted, if not on the expert's personal knowledge or observation, it must be given on hypothetical questions encompassing only factors which are in evidence . . . Therefore, in order to minimize the increasing publicity of the trial, the court had Dr. DeBakey questioned in chambers with all counsel present and a court reporter. The record will amply reveal that Dr. DeBakey had not been employed to give any expert medical opinion; that he would not accept any employment in this case; that he had never examined Mr. Karp; that he had never seen Mr. Karp; that he would refuse to express any medical opinion concerning the treatment of Mr. Karp; that he would not express any medical opinion based upon hypothetical questions even if asked to do so; and in connection with the Cooley–Liotta mechanical heart used in Mr. Karp, he would refuse to express an in–court expert opinion concerning that device. Accordingly, this court concluded that Dr. DeBakey had no evidence of any probative value to present to the jury. Accordingly, to allow the plaintiff's attorney to call Dr. DeBakey as a witness before the jury under such circumstances would in all reasonable probability result in creating a highly prejudicial and inflammatory situation that would serve no useful purpose.

Dr. DeBakey was served with a subpoena with twenty dollars attached thereto by the plaintiffs' attorney. Dr. DeBakey appeared in court and at that time returned the twenty dollars to plaintiff's attorney . . . The various rules on compelling an expert to testify, in the absence of statutory provision, are affected by such factors as the nature of the action or proceeding in which the expert is called as a witness, by the nature or subject of the testimony, or by the status, relationship, or situation of the party by or against whom the testimony is sought. Thus, in some cases, the rule of compulsion has been limited to criminal prosecutions, and has been held not invocable by or on behalf of a private litigant.

In the absence of any statutory provision, this court weighed the factors set out above and determined that Dr. DeBakey could not be compelled to testify . . .

The defendants were also charged with fraudulent representations in connection with the written consent executed before Mr. Karp's operation. Fraudulent representations may assume three forms: 1) a false representation concerning a past or existing fact; 2) a promise made with a present intention not to perform; and 3) a statement of opinion made with the intent to deceive. In order for a representation to be fraudulent, the jury would necessarily have had to find the following elements:

a. Defendants made the representation;

b. The representation was made concerning past or existing facts;

c. The representation was communicated to Haskell Karp in this case. In that connection such representation may be communicated through an individual or individuals who are not parties to the lawsuit;

d. The past or existing facts referred to in (b) above were material to the transaction and susceptible of knowledge on the part of defendants;

e. The representation was false at the time it was made;

f. The representation was made with the intent to induce Haskell Karp to do or refrain from doing some act (i.e., signing the consent);

g. The representation was relied upon by Haskell Karp in that Haskell Karp believed it to be true and was induced to act or refrain from acting thereby and Haskell Karp would not have acted upon or refrained from acting in the absence of such representation. It is not necessary that the defendants knew that such representation was false in order to find that the representation was fraudulent.

    h. Haskell Karp suffered damage or injury as a result.

A promise may also amount to fraudulent representation if the defendants made the promise with the intention, design, and purpose of deceiving and of not performing the promise. In addition, of course, each and all of the elements enumerated in paragraphs a through h, above, must be found by the jury. In the case of such a false promise, the law considers the state of mind of the defendants to constitute an existing fact.

A statement of opinion may also amount to a fraudulent representation. In order for a statement of opinion to amount to a fraudulent representation, the jury must find that the opinion was made with the intention, design, and purpose of deceiving and that the defendants did not believe the opinion so expressed. In addition, of course, each and all of the elements enumerated in paragraphs a through h, above, must be found by the jury. In the case of such a statement of opinion, the law considers the state of mind of defendants to constitute an existing fact.

The evidence produced at trial was not of such quality and weight . . . to raise a fact issue for the jury on fraudulent representations, promises, or opinions. Likewise, no proximate causation could have been found from any of the alleged representations and Mr. Karp's death . . .

There was no proof showing that any statement, promise, or opinions made by Dr. Cooley resulted in Haskell Karp's death and, therefore, any injury to plaintiffs . . .

This same theory of proximate cause would have to have been applied to any issue of malpractice regarding the technical aspects of the surgeries themselves. The Texas law is clear that the court and jury must rely on expert testimony to determine negligence. "There can be no other guide, and where want of skill and attention is not thus shown by expert evidence applied to the facts, there is no evidence of it proper to be submitted to the jury. . . .

In determining proximate cause, the proof must be beyond a showing of possibility that the injuries arose from the defendant's negligence or lack of skill, since a jury may not speculate as to the cause of the injury.

In summary, the requirement is to show through testimony of expert medical witnesses of the same school that the doctor's act did in fact cause injury not that it was a sole proximate cause . . . Since there was no expert evidence that the doctors had performed any act negligently nor that any of their acts were a proximate cause of Mr. Karp's death, a directed verdict for both defendants must be entered . . .

o **Recap of the Case.** Nurses may become extremely concerned when they observe that patients are about to take action which may be harmful to them. When nurses become aware of this possibility, they should bear in mind the principles of this case. As long as patients understand the possible consequences of their actions, practitioners will not be liable when injury or death results.

PATIENT NOT CONTRIBUTORILY NEGLIGENT FOR SELF-ADMINISTRATION OF NARCOTICS

Contributory negligence on the part of the plaintiff is also a complete defense to a claim of negligence in many states. Contributory negligence is conduct by the plaintiff which causes harm to the plaintiff because the conduct falls below the standard required for his own protection. In *Los Alamos Medical Center, Inc. v. Coe*, 58 N.M.686, 257 P.2d 175 (1954), the defendant practitioner permitted the plaintiff to self-administer morphine for pain at home. The plaintiff did so, became addicted, and charged the physician with negligence. Since the plaintiff admitted that she had administered morphine to help her "feel good" even when she was not in pain, the defendant claimed that the plaintiff was contributorily negligent.

Los Alamos Medical Center, Inc. v. Coe,
58 N.M. 686, 275 P.2d 175 (1954)
Supreme Court of New Mexico

. . . Mrs. Coe was admitted to the hospital on several occasions. On March 28, 1950, she was admitted for dilation and curettage. She again entered the hospital April 16, 1950 for similar treatment. On June 6, 1950, she was admitted for a major operation, separation of adhesions and supra-vaginal hysterectomy. The latter operation was performed by appellant. Subsequently, on June 13, 1950, she entered the hospital for removal of intestinal obstructions and was finally discharged therefrom July 15, 1950. During all this time she received narcotics in some form or another. It seems Dr.

Behney did not perform the latter operation, nevertheless, Mrs. Coe again became his patient on July 25 and remained such until November 3, 1950, at which time she went to Los Angeles, California and entered the Good Samaritan Hospital in Los Angeles, California, where she was diagnosed as a morphine addict after surgery. The amount, kind and quantity of narcotics prescribed and used by Mrs. Coe as shown by the hospital records is as follows:

Date	Drug	Dose	Quantity	Doctor
3–28–50	Demerol	.05	12	Shafer
4–4–50	"	.05	3	Behney
4–8–50				
4–14–50	Codein	.061	12	Behney
4–15–50	Demerol	.05	3	Behney
4–18–50	M.S.	.011	10	Behney
4–18–50	Codein	.032	10	Behney
4–21–50	M.S.	.011	10	Behney
4–25–50	M.S.	.011	12	Behney
4–27–50	" "	.011	12	Behney
4–27–50	Demerol	.05	30	Behney
5–2–50	M.S.	.011	12	Behney
5–24–50	" "	.014	6	Shafer
5–26–50	" "	.016	6	Hawley
6–6–50				
6–13–50				
7–22–50	M.S.	.008	10	Wilcox
7–28–50	" "	.011	20	Behney
8–2–50	" "	gr.1/6	20	Behney
8–5–50	Demerol	.05	30	Behney
8–6–50	M.S.	gr.1/6	20	Hawley
8–11–50	" "	gr.1/6	20	Hawley
8–15–50	" "	gr.1/6	15	Hawley
8–17–50	" "	.011	20	Behney
8–25–50	" "	.011	20	Behney
8–28–50	" "	.011	20	Behney
8–28–50	Codein (APC)	.032	20	Behney
9–1–50	M.S.	.011	20	Behney
9–5–50	" "	.011	20	Behney
9–5–50	Codein (APC)	.032	30	Behney
9–8–50	M.S.	.011	20	Behney
9–12–50	" "	.011	20	Behney
9–20–50	" "	.011	20	Behney
9–23–50	" "	.011	20	Behney

Date	Drug	Dose	Quantity	Doctor
9-27-50	" "	.011	20	Behney
9-29-50	M.S.	.011	20	Behney
10-2-50	" "	.011	20	Behney
10-5-50	" "	.011	20	Behney
10-7-50	M.S. Sol	20cc-.210		Behney
10-12-50	" "	20cc-G.210		Behney
10-16-50	" "	20cc-200		Behney
10-18-50	" "	20cc-.194		Behney
10-23-50	" "	20cc-.194		Behney
10-26-50	" "	20cc-.194		Behney
10-27-50	" "	20cc-.194		Behney
10-31-50	" "	20cc-.194		Behney

As previously stated, Mrs. Coe became Dr. Behney's patient on July 25, 1950, the date she was discharged from the Medical Center. After returning to her home she began to complain of severe pains and appellees consulted Dr. Behney about self-administration of narcotics at home and this was agreeable to Dr. Behney. The husband, son, daughter, son-in-law, and Mrs. Coe herself, all administered morphine to her by hypodermic injections. Actually, from July 25, 1950 to November 3, 1950, Dr. Behney made no calls to their home nor did he treat her organic trouble except to make two or three pelvic examinations. When she would complain of pain, they would phone appellant and he would issue a prescription for morphine to be administered for relief of pain as needed, and they were to be the judge in this respect. This continued until the Coes themselves decided that she was not recovering properly from her organic trouble and they decided to call a Dr. Norris of Los Angeles and to ask his advice concerning her progress. Dr. Norris advised her to contact Dr. Cornish of Albuquerque, which she did. Subsequently, about November 1, 1950, the Coes decided to go to Los Angeles for further consultation with Dr. Norris. They discussed the matter with Dr. Behney, who advised them it was unnecessary as her recovery was satisfactory, nevertheless, he agreed, and on November 2, 1950, Dr. Behney gave her an additional 30 morphine tablets and 36 sleeping pills to tide her over until she could contact Dr. Norris. This prescription is not shown on the above chart. She left Albuquerque November 3, 1950 by plane and was admitted to the Good Samaritan Hospital the following day. She then complained of great pain, requiring an unusual amount of morphine. Dr. Norris performed an exploratory operation on November 13 and found her to be suffering from adhesions and intestinal obstructions and apparently experiencing pain. Following the operation, her tolerance to pain was so low as to arouse Dr. Norris' suspicion as to her use of narcotics. It was found she had been using morphine about every three hours, day and night, but having utmost confidence in Dr. Norris, Mrs. Coe confided in him the amount of morphine she had taken and at his demand agreed to undertake the withdrawal, which followed. The operation performed by him was successful and she was discharged from the hospital December 7, 1950. The agonies of her withdrawal were related to the jury by Dr. Norris and Mrs. Coe. This evidence warrants an inference of addiction due to the lack of care on the part of appellant. Instead of attempting to discover the cause of her suffering and relieving it, Dr. Behney continually gave her morphine to relieve her pain and desires, with the result, as the jury found, she became an addict . . .

The Coes themselves were apprehensive and discussed the possibility of addiction with appellant and he assured them that they had no cause for alarm as her pain was so severe that it would counteract the effect of the morphine. He was thus put on notice but remained indifferent as to the harmful results which followed. We think this evidence was sufficient to take that issue to the jury.

Mrs. Coe's deposition was taken December 18, 1951, in which she stated that she felt she became an addict while in the hospital, the latter part of June or the first part of July, 1950. Appellant excepted to all testimony concerning the use of morphine by her subsequent to that date, claiming she is bound by her answer. There is no merit to this contention. Both Dr. Norris and Dr. Cornish testified that a person could not testify with any degree of certainty when he becomes an addict. The testimony of the medical experts on the subject should be controlling.

Appellant seriously questions the qualifications of Dr. Norris and Dr. Cornish to express an opinion as to the addiction of Mrs. Coe. Both are general practitioners of medicine and surgery, Dr. Norris in California and Dr. Cornish in Albuquerque. A graduate of a well recognized Medical College, Dr. Cornish has been engaged in general practice in Albuquerque since 1920. During the course of his practice, he has administered morphine and also encountered drug addiction in the treatment of his patients. He testified it was a simple matter to detect whether a patient is addicted to the use of narcotics. Actually, he testified that while he was not an expert in that field, he had taken courses in the treatment, care and detention of addicts. The mere fact that he may have had no particular experience in the immediate vicinity of Los Alamos in the use of morphine, does not render his testimony inadmissible. The standard of care and skill required of physicians in administering morphine unquestionably is the same. Dr. Norris has practiced his profession for some 32 years. Licensed in New York, California and Arizona, he is a senior member of surgical staffs of several hospitals, and while not claiming to be an expert on the subject of narcotics, has observed many addicts and actually treated several cases. He likewise stated it is a simple matter to determine if a patient is addicted. We think they were competent to testify though they may not be highly qualified to testify on the subject.

Specialists in drug addiction testified on behalf of appellant to the effect that the quantity of drugs shown to have been administered to Mrs. Coe could not result in addiction and that the withdrawal of a true addict could not be accomplished within the short time required for withdrawal by Mrs. Coe. We have already held that the expert testimony of Dr. Norris and Dr. Cornish, expressing a different view, was admissible. Under these circumstances, it was within the province of the jury to evaluate and choose between the views of the experts on this question, and we are not in a position to disturb the jury's finding of addiction.

Appellant urges that appellees are guilty of contributory negligence and assumed the risk incident to the use of the morphine by them . . .

> Negligence of the patient, to constitute a bar to the suit, must have been an active and efficient contributing cause of the injury; it must have been simultaneous and co-operating with the fault of the defendant, must have entered into the creation of the cause of action, and have been an element in the transaction which constituted it. Where the fault of the patient was subsequent to the fault of the physician and merely aggravated the injury inflicted by the physician, it only affects the amount of the damages recoverable by the patient. Since the patient may rely on the directions of his physician, it follows that he incurs no liability by doing so. . . .

The evidence is clear that Mrs. Coe in order to get a prescription, frequently complained of pain when no pain was present. She testified she used it at the last for the jitters and for nervousness, at other times just to feel good. But being fearful of its harmful effects, appellees contacted appellant as to the consequences of using too much morphine and were told by him not to worry in this regard as Mrs. Coe was improving physically and that she could be given morphine whenever she felt the need of it. Appellees testified they relied upon the instructions of appellant in this regard. Obviously they had a right to rely upon his superior knowledge . . .

The judgment will be affirmed with direction to the lower court to enter judgment against appellant and the surety upon his supersedeas bond, and it is so ordered.

o Recap of the Case. The patient in this case was allowed to self-administer morphine. She did so whether or not she was in pain and subsequently became addicted. She then sued the practitioner who permitted her to do this, claiming negligence. The defendant responded and claimed that the patient was contributorily negligent because she self-administered narcotics even when she was not in pain. The court ruled against the defendant primarily because the physician was contacted regarding the dangers of self-administration and said there was nothing to be concerned about. Even though the court rejected the defendant's argument of contributory negligence in this case, nurses should remember that actions taken by the patient may relieve them of liability altogether.

PATIENT'S MALPRACTICE SUIT DISMISSED BECAUSE FILED MORE THAN TWO YEARS AFTER INJURY OCCURRED

Statutes of limitations set forth time periods within which a malpractice suit must be filed. If the suit is not filed within the required time period, it will not be allowed by the courts. While statutes of limitations vary from state to state, most provide that suit be brought within two or three years. It is sometimes very difficult to determine when this statutory period begins. Some states have determined that the period begins when the negligent treatment is performed. A number of other states have adopted the so-called "discovery rule," which requires that the period begin when the plaintiff discovers the injury or should have discovered the injury. In still other states, the period begins when the treatment or physician-patient relationship is terminated. In some states, if the patient is a minor when the negligence occurs, the period begins when the patient reaches the age of majority. However, if the negligence is fraudulently concealed, the statutory period does not begin until the discovery of that negligence.

In *Hill v. Hays*, 1983 Kan. 443, 395 P.2d 298 (1964), plaintiff suffered an acromio–clavicular separation of his left shoulder in a motorcycle accident. Defendant made several attempts to repair the injury without success, and the Plaintiff sued.

A statute in effect in Kansas at that time required plaintiffs to sue within two years from the time the injury occurred or lose their right to sue altogether. Plaintiff filed suit after the two–year time period had elapsed, but argued that the time for filing his suit was extended because the physician–patient relationship continued beyond the date when injury occurred. The court rejected this argument and dismissed the plaintiff's suit.

Hill v. Hays, 193 Kan. 443, 395 P.2d 298 (1964)
Supreme Court of Kansas

. . . The plaintiff, a man twenty–nine years of age, was involved in a motorcycle accident on May 28, 1960. He suffered an injury to his left shoulder known as an acromio–clavicular separation, the outward physical appearance being a knot on the end of his shoulder. Plaintiff consulted defendant relative to treatment of his injury. The defendant assured plaintiff that he was competent to repair plaintiff's injured shoulder and undertook the treatment of the injury sustained. The care and treatment took place from May 28, 1960, through August 27, 1960.

The treatment consisted of inserting a pin through his shoulder attempting to hold the acromio–clavicular joint in position. The pin was inserted on May 29, 1960, and broke on or about June 20, 1960. On or about June 30, 1960, a second and larger pin was inserted in plaintiff's shoulder. Thereafter an infection developed in the plaintiff's arm as a result of the intrusion of the second pin and the pin was removed about the last week in July, 1960.

. . . Thereafter, the defendant continued treating the plaintiff, the exact nature of the treatment the plaintiff does not know but occasioned visits to the Doctor's office at the Doctor's request on six occasions thereafter, the last one being on August 27, 1960, at which time plaintiff was advised he could return to work on August 29th and to return back to the Doctor's office in two weeks. Immediately upon removal of the pin, a knot still remained on the plaintiff's left shoulder the same as at the time he consulted defendant for treatment, but that defendant stated to the plaintiff that his shoulder would be just as strong or even stronger than ever. In truth and in fact said injury did not heal, has not healed, and remains in the same general condition it was in when the plaintiff sought the services of the defendant in the treatment of the said injury . . .

The amended petition alleged that the defendant was negligent in treating the injury in the following respects:

A. The failure to establish a ligament between the clavical and the coracoid process.
B. Failure to reduce the dislocation of the acromio–clavical joint.
C. Using improper size of pin and using only a pin to hold joint in position without reestablishment of ligaments to hold joint in place after removal of pin.
D. Failure to properly sterilize pin used and disinfect the shoulder resulting in infection and pus forming around the second pin . . .

Approaching the more substantial issues it is agreed that a malpractice action is based on negligence and governed by the provisions of G.S. 1949, 60–306, *Third*, which limits the commencement of such an action to two years after the cause of action shall have accrued, i.e., when the negligent act occurred.

Appellant contends that the statute of limitations did not commence to run on his cause of action until the relationship of patient and physician relative to the particular injury and treatment had ceased to exist.

Appellant cites numerous cases from other jurisdictions in support of his contention. Without analysing the numerous cases cited, it must be conceded that appellant's contention is supported by considerable authority. However, it does not appear to be the general rule . . . It has never been the law in this state. This court has adhered to the rule that the cause of action accrues and the statute of limitations begins to run on an action for malpractice at the time the tort is committed. The time in which the action must be brought is not tolled by the fact that the relationship of physician and patient continues to exist . . .

This court may not approve of the law announced above, however, it does not make the law as to the limitation of time in which an action may be brought . . . Limitations are created by statute and are legislative, not judicial acts . . .

The legislature has specifically stated that the statute of limitations begins to run on an action such as is now before us when the cause of action accrues . . .

We are forced to conclude that any charge of negligence based on either acts of commission or acts of omission which occurred prior to August 27, 1960, is barred by the statute of limitations, and the limitation of time in which action may be brought is not extended by the fact that the relationship of physician and patient may have continued for a limited time thereafter, in this case only one day.

The appellant further contends that its action was filed August 27, 1962, and that the statute of limitations did not bar an action for negligence which occurred on August 27, 1960. Appellant argues:

. . . Plaintiff contends it was defendant's duty as a physician to render to plaintiff the necessary professional services needed to treat and repair plaintiff's injury; that this duty existed on May 28, 1960 and continued to exist until at least August 27, 1960, when the plaintiff was released by the defendant to return to work on August 29, 1960; that it was a continuing negligence on the part of the defendant to leave plaintiff's injured shoulder in the same condition during all the time plaintiff was under the care and treatment of the defendant when said injury could have been corrected and repaired had the defendant not been negligent in his treatment of plaintiff's injury. . . .

We do not believe the appellant's argument leaves him sufficient ground on which to stand. If appellee's negligence consisted of not having corrected the injury on August 27, 1960, it was the duty of the defendant to return for further attention as directed. No specific acts of negligence are charged as occurring on August 27, 1960. There could be no negligent acts on that day unless they are assumed from the failure to obtain a complete remedy of the injury on the specific date.

Negligence of a physician cannot be presumed from mere failure to obtain the best results from an operation or treatment . . .

If the best results had not been obtained in treating appellant's injury on August 27, 1960, there being no specific acts of negligence alleged as of that date, the negligence acts of commission or omission, if any, must have occurred prior thereto.

We must conclude, as did the trial court, that the petition shows on its face that any cause of action attempted to be stated was barred by the statute of limitations and the demurrer to the petition was properly sustained.

The judgment is affirmed.

o Recap of the Case. Time limits for filing malpractice cases are usually established by statute in the legislature in each state. Consequently, these time limits vary from state to state. It is thus up to the courts in each state to interpret these statutes of limitation. The statute in effect in Kansas at the time this case was tried stated that malpractice suits had to be brought within two years of the date upon which the injury occurred. The patient sued more than two years after the injury occurred, but argued that the suit should not be dismissed because his relationship with the defendant continued beyond the date of injury. The court rejected this exception and dismissed the suit.

PRACTITIONER LIABLE ALTHOUGH SUIT FILED MORE THAN TWO YEARS AFTER INJURY OCCURRED

In *Frohs v. Green*, 452 P.2d 564 (Ore. 1969), the plaintiff received injections from the defendant which injured her. In response to her complaints about resulting pain, the defendant assured her that there would be no further difficulties.

A statute in effect at that time required plaintiffs to sue for malpractice within two years of the injury. But the plaintiff in this case did not even learn of defendant's negligence until after the two-year period expired. Nevertheless, the court did not dismiss her suit. Instead, it applied the discovery rule which allows plaintiffs to sue within two years of the date they become aware of or should have known of the defendant's negligence. The plaintiff in this case met this requirement.

Frohs v. Green, 452 P.2d 564 (Ore. 1969)
Supreme Court of Oregon

. . . Plaintiff filed her complaint on May 10, 1967, alleging that in 1951 defendants negligently gave her injections of penicillin when they knew or should have known that plaintiff was allergic to penicillin. She also alleged that defendants were negligent in failing to take certain treatment to counter the injections.

Plaintiff contends that the statute of limitations did not begin to run until plaintiff discovered or in the exercise of reasonable care should have discovered that she had been tortiously injured by defendants. Defendants contend that the application of the discovery rule in medical malpractice cases should be limited to cases where foreign objects are negligently left in patients' bodies at the completion of operations. This court adopted the discovery rule in foreign object cases . . . The question is whether [this rule] should be extended to cases of negligent diagnosis or treatment.

Defendants argue that such an extension of the rule would open great opportunities for fraudulent claims and would subject physicians to an intolerable burden of defending stale claims at a time when any practical opportunity for an actual recollection of the facts and circumstances had elapsed. Defendants point out that the existence of a foreign object in the body is an intrinsic attestation to the reliability, of the proof of a negligent act and its relationship to the injury. This reliability, they claim, is not present in claims for negligent treatment or diagnosis . . .

On a theoretical basis it is impossible to justify the applicability of the discovery rule to one kind of malpractice and not to another. The reason for the application of the discovery rule is the same in each instance. It is manifestly unrealistic and unfair to bar a negligently injured party's cause of action before he has had an opportunity to discover that it exists. This is true whether it consists of faulty diagnosis or treatment . . . We do not believe that the danger of spurious claims is so great as to necessitate the infliction of injustice on persons having legitimate claims which were undiscoverable by the exercise of ordinary care prior to the lapse of two years from the time of the act inflicting the injury. Nor do we believe the legislature intended such a result . . .

The allegations of plaintiff's complaint are as follows:

Within a short time after such injections, plaintiff experienced severe pains, but was assured by defendants that any possible problems connected with the injection of penicillin had been counteracted and would give rise to no further difficulty. Such symptoms were complex and plaintiff was required and did seek further treatment from defendants, as well as other physicians and medical personnel in an effort to find alternative explanations for her illnesses. Defendant doctors, when consulted by plaintiff, still continued to assure her that the penicillin injections given her in 1951 were in no way causing her difficulties. The other doctors and medical personnel with whom plaintiff consulted and who are not defendants, did not participate in the 1951 procedures (and for this reason did not have the benefit of the first hand information available to defendants) were not able to determine the cause of her difficulties. Plaintiff diligently and continously sought to determine the alternative cause of her physical difficulties. It was not until May 11, 1965, when surgery was performed within plaintiff's temple, that it was first shown that her problems were attributable to defendant's negligent treatment in 1951. Such representations by defendants were material and plaintiff at all times relied thereon and had no reason to believe, and did not believe, the facts were otherwise until said surgery in 1965. Defendants' representations had the effect of preventing plaintiff from consulting other physicians to determine if the penicillin injections were responsible for her inability to discover the true cause. Defendants either knew that such representations were untrue or knew that they did not have sufficient information with which to make such statements at the time they were made. Many of the other doctors whom plaintiff consulted were specialists in fields other than those in which defendants practiced. Defendants intended that plaintiff act upon such representations in the manner in which she did. As a result of such reliance, plaintiff sustained . . .

Plaintiff has alleged that she first discovered that she was suffering from defendants' negligent treatment on May 11, 1965. This action was begun on May 10, 1967, which was within two years of the alleged discovery. Her action was, therefore, timely filed, provided that her allegations were sufficient to show that in the exercise of reasonable diligence she should not have discovered previously that defendants had committed a tort upon her body in 1951.

She alleged that shortly after the injections she was assured by defendants that her physical difficulties were not caused by the injections and that these assurances were continued by defendants' doctors during her treatment by defendants. She also alleged that the representations by defendants had the effect of preventing her from consulting other doctors. She indicates, however, that she did consult other doctors and they were unable to determine the cause of her difficulties until the operation of May 11, 1965. We believe that the above allegations would normally be sufficient to show that, in the exercise of reasonable diligence, she should not have discovered that she had a cause of action.

However, plaintiff also alleged that she was told that possible problems connected with the injections "had been counteracted" and would cause "no further difficulties." The quoted language can only be consistent with her possession of knowledge that she might have received some adverse effects from the injections. While the complaint is not a model of clarity, we construe it to say that plaintiff was told by defendants that the "severe pains" she experienced shortly after the injections were not attributable to them, and that possible problems which had been counteracted referred to other difficulties she must have experienced prior to the time she complained to the doctor of her severe pains. This raises the question whether the statute commenced to run when plaintiff became aware that the difficulty she had prior to the severe pains was attributable to the injections.

Normally, knowledge of injury as the result of defendants' actions would put the injured party on sufficient notice of defendants' tortious conduct to commence the running of the statute. However, immediate, adverse side effects commonly result from medical treatment given to gain long-range and more important benefits. Knowledge of momentary, adverse effects which are immediately controlled would not put plaintiff on notice as a matter of law of tortious conduct by defendants. It may be that, upon trial, the facts will indicate that she did have such notice. However, we do not believe that the allegations of the complaint are sufficient for the court to say that as a matter of law the statute has run.

We conclude that plaintiff has sufficiently alleged non-discovery of defendants' claimed malpractice as well as sufficient facts to show that in the exercise of reasonable diligence she should not have discovered such malpractice prior to the date of her operation.

The judgment of the trial court is reversed and the case is remanded for further proceedings.

o **Recap of the Case.** The Frohs case provides an example of a common exception to the discovery rule. Sometimes patients do not actually know or could not have known of their injury within the time period established by the statute of limitations. In these cases, courts will often extend the period for filing a suit for the number of years provided in the statute beginning with the date that the patient actually knew or should have known of the injury.

PRACTITIONER LIABLE FOR INJURY WHICH OCCURRED TWENTY-TWO YEARS BEFORE SUIT WAS FILED

In *Chaffin v. Nicosia*, 261 Ind. 698, 310 N.E.2d 867 (1974), the plaintiff sued within two years after he reached adulthood for injuries occurring at birth. These injuries resulted in a significant loss of eyesight. The defendants argued that the plaintiff failed to file his claim within the statute of limitations, which expired two years after the injuries were sustained. The court ruled in the plaintiff's favor primarily to avoid potentially harsh and inequitable results such as the dismissal of plaintiff's complaints in situations such as Chaffin's.

Chaffin v. Nicosia, 261 Ind. 698, 310 N.E.2d 867 (1974)
Supreme Court of Indiana

This cause arises upon petition to transfer and presents two issues for our determination:

(1) Whether a statute allowing medical practitioners the special privilege of a two-year time period within which they may be sued is violative of Article I, § 23 of the Constitution of Indiana;

(2) Whether the two-year statute of limitations for medical malpractice is an exception to, or in irreconcilable conflict with, a statute allowing minors to sue within two years after reaching majority.

Appellant's complaint alleged medical malpractice on the part of appellee arising from appellee's treatment of appellant's mother during her pregnancy and during appellant's birth. More specifically, the complaint alleged the following:

During 1941, Marjory Chaffin became pregnant and employed Nicosia to care for her through the pregnancy and the birth of the child. She had suffered a prior miscarriage of which Nicosia was aware. He advised her that she would also have trouble carrying this child.

Approximately four days prior to August 28, 1942, Marjory Chaffin began to have labor pains. Nicosia advised her that he would not do anything until he took x–rays to determine Ronald's position in the womb. Nicosia, however, failed to take the x–rays, failed to prescribe medication, and failed to take any other positive action.

Marjory Chaffin remained in labor for approximately seventy–two hours, and Ronald was finally born on August 28, 1942. During the delivery process, Nicosia used foceps on both sides of Ronald's head, near his eyes. There were large areas of discoloration on both sides of Ronald's head for several days after birth. For more than one year, he also had dents on both sides of the head. As a result of the way Nicosia used the forceps, Ronald's optic nerve controlling his right eye was severely damaged, resulting in an almost complete loss of eyesight in his right eye. This loss of eyesight continues to the present.

The instant action was filed on August 27, 1965, within two years of appellant's reaching majority . . .

The trial court sustained appellee's motion since the transaction at issue had occurred twenty–two years prior to the filing of the complaint . . .

Appellant urges here that the medical malpractice statute is unconstitutional on its face in that it grants special privileges and immunities to medical professionals which do not equally belong to all citizens. . .

The question of classification under the above section is primarily a question for the legislature. Legislative classification becomes a judicial question only where the lines drawn appear arbitrary or manifestly unreasonable. So long as the classification is based upon substantial distinctions with reference to the subject matter, we will not substitute our judgment for that of the legislature; nor will we inquire into the legislative motives prompting such classification . . .

The classification at issue does not appear unconstitutional *per se*. There exists a reasonable basis for distinguishing between those rendering medical services and those who do not. Appellant has failed in his burden of showing in what way the two-year limitation period unduly discriminates in favor of medical practitioners . . .

However, a determination that a statute is constitutionally valid on its face does not end judicial inquiry into its application to particular facts. The limitations statute before us admits of no exceptions: *An action is barred unless brought within two years of the act complained of* . . .

Recognizing that a literal application of this limitation would result in possible inequity, this Court held . . . that fraudulent concealment would toll the medical malpractice statute.

Similarly . . . we held that the medical malpractice statute would not apply retroactively to bar a minor's claim arising from neglect occurring prior to passage of the act.

. . . To construe the medical malpractice statute as a legislative bar on all malpractice actions under all circumstances unless commenced within two years from the act complained of (discoverable or otherwise) would raise substantial questions under the guarantee of open courts and redress for injury to every man, not to mention the offense to lay concepts of justice.

The potentially harsh results under the Court of Appeals opinion should not be ignored. This is perhaps the most compelling argument in favor of the appellant's position. Unless the malpractice act, omission, or neglect complained of happens to occur within two years of the minor's reaching his majority, he may effectively be deprived of his cause of action. This extraordinarily harsh result would be particularly inconsistent with the legislature's intention in creating this particular legal disability—that is, the protection of minors.

This construction of the statutes at issue in the case at bar is founded upon the only logical basis. It makes practical sense particularly with respect to infants who, because of their youth, cannot be expected to articulate their physical and mental conditions or to realize and act timely to preserve their rights. It is not difficult to conceive of situations where the results of medical malpractice upon an infant could remain undiscovered for a number of years . . .

Reversed and remanded.

o **Recap of the Case.** This case provides another example of an exception to the strict application of the statute of limitations. Specifically, if injury occurred while the patient was a minor, the courts in some jurisdictions will extend the period of time for filing for a specified number of years from the date the patient becomes an adult. The basis for this exception is the obligation of the courts to provide special protection for minors who are unable to initiate malpractice suits themselves until they become adults.

FRAUD OR CONCEALMENT OF NEGLIGENCE EXTENDS THE PERIOD OF TIME FOR FILING MALPRACTICE SUIT

In *Baurer v. Bowen*, 63 N.J. Super. 225, 164 A.2d 357 (1960), the plaintiff had an abortion, or at least that is what she claimed the defendant physician told her. Fifteen days later, she expelled a portion of the fetus thereby alerting her to the fact that the abortion performed earlier was either done improperly or not at all. She returned to his offices immediately, at which time the defendant performed a "D & C." The plaintiff sued the defendant within two years of the discovery of defendant's negligence, but more than two years after the injury occurred. Nevertheless, the court concluded that she could continue to pursue her suit because the defendant committed fraud when he told her the procedure was completed, when it was not adequately done. In cases of fraud or concealment of negligence, the plaintiff may sue two years from the date of discovery of the injury or two years from the date the injury should have been discovered by the plaintiff.

Baurer v. Bowen, 63 N.J. Super. 225, 164 A.2d 357 (1960)
New Jersey Superior Court

. . . We need concern ourselves on this appeal only with the first count of the amended complaint, which charges both negligence and fraud, in its relationship to the statute of limitations. The amended complaint filed on March 30, 1959 does not set forth a new cause of action, but the same cause of action in somewhat different form. Therefore, the time of its filing relates back to the time of the filing of the original complaint on March 23, 1959 and the latter governs.

The applicable statute of limitations in a suit for personal injuries based upon the alleged malpractice of a doctor, provides:

Every action at law for an injury to the person caused by the wrongful act, neglect or default of any person within this state shall be commenced within 2 years next after the cause of any such action shall be accrued.

The important issue on this appeal is when did the plaintiff's cause of action "accrue". It was conceded on the oral argument that the defendant operated on the female plaintiff on March 6, 1957, performing a lawful, therapeutic abortion. His answer denies her charge of fraud, so that the pleadings raise an issue of fact as to whether he falsely represented that he had completely removed the foetus in the operation. Her complaint alleges that she imposed a trust in him and believed in him and relied upon his superior means of information as to what had been done to her body. The respective briefs concede that she remained at the hospital under his care until March 16, 1957, when she was discharged and returned to her home. On March 21, 1957, while the female plaintiff was at home, there appeared from her body a part of the foetus, which would establish the falsity of his representations, if he ever made them. Plaintiff was immediately transported back to the hospital. The defendant was called, came to the hospital, and on March 22, 1957 performed what is known as a "D & C," a scraping of the uterus.

If the statute of limitations is to be computed from March 6, 1957, when the defendant allegedly performed a negligent operation, then obviously the complaint filed on March 23, 1959, or the amended complaint, was not within the time limitation fixed by the statute. On the other hand, if the cause of action *accrued* on March 21, 1957, when the female plaintiff discovered that the defendant had perpetrated the alleged fraud, or if it accrued on March 22, 1957 when the defendant last treated the female plaintiff, then the suit would have been within time.

It must be observed at this point that March 21 and March 22, 1959 were respectively a Saturday and a Sunday. [The] statute provides that when the last day prescribed by law for an act to be done falls on a Saturday, or a Sunday, or a legal holiday, when the public offices are closed to transactions of business, if the act is done on the next day when the public office is open, it is done within time. Therefore, a filing of the complaint on Monday, March 23, 1959 would be within time, if it is concluded that plaintiffs' cause of action accrued either on March 21, or March 22, 1957.

Generally, by New Jersey case decisions, in a malpractice action, where an operation has been performed, the statute of limitations begins to run from the day of the negligent performance of the operation, even though the negligence of the doctor may not be discovered until some time thereafter . . .

However, two exceptions to the foregoing fundamental rule were listed. First, if injurious consequences arise from a continuing course of *negligent* treatment, the statute does not ordinarily begin to run until the treatment is terminated, unless the patient shall have earlier discovered the injury. The allegations of the amended complaint do not bring this case within that exception. If the defendant were guilty of any negligence, it would have been on March 6, 1957, when the operation was allegedly negligently performed. There is no valid assertion of any continuing course of *negligent* treatment thereafter. Apparently there was none, since what was done on March 22, 1957 by the defendant doctor was corrective, properly done, and not negligent.

The second exception to the basic rule covers a situation where "the physician is guilty of fraudulent concealment." Then the statute is tolled pending discovery of the fraud. The amended complaint in this case charges fraudulent representations and fraudulent concealment of the truth from plaintiffs, viz., that the female plaintiff had been informed by defendant that the foetus had been completely removed in the course of the abortion operation, when in fact that was false, and that the truth was concealed from her, until her own discovery of March 21, 1957. We do not pass on the truth of her asserted claim. The exception to the statute of limitations rule is controlling here. The trial court should not have dismissed the amended complaint, as barred by the statute of limitations, because it contained within its allegations a charge of fraud by the defendant and non–discovery of the truth by the female plaintiff until March 21, 1957 . . .

o **Recap of the Case.** The *Baurer* case is another example of an exception frequently made to time periods established by statutes of limitation. If the practitioner conceals the negligence from the patient, courts in some jurisdictions will extend the period of time for filing, starting with the date the patient knew or should have known of the practitioner's negligence.

GENERAL RELEASE RELIEVES ALL DEFENDANTS FROM LIABILITY

A release is a binding document for the purpose of preventing a plaintiff from taking any further action concerning the alleged claims of negligence. In other words, plaintiffs who sign releases will not be able to sue the defendant later for injuries resulting from the negligent act covered by the release. A difficult issue which arises in connection with the use of releases is whether or not a release drafted in general terms includes individuals who are not specifically named in the release but who are involved in the negligent conduct. Although most states require specificity in the release, some states have adopted the reasoning of *Whitt v. Hutchinson*, 43 Ohio St.2d 53, 330 N.E.2d 678 (1975), in which the court held that a release containing only general language will release specific practitioners from liability.

Whitt v. Hutchinson, 43 Ohio St.2d 53, 330 N.E.2d 678 (1975)
Supreme Court of Ohio

. . . The difficulties and injustices of common–law rules regarding the effect of releases have been replaced in this state by principles of law which permit an injured party to settle that injury and action as he may intend. The effect of such a settlement upon the rights and obligations of others who might also be jointly liable for the injury is established . . .

At common law, the traditional rule was that a general release executed in favor of one charged with a wrong extinguished the right of action against all those jointly liable for the same wrong. The somewhat metaphysical theory of this rule is that for a single injury there is a single, indivisible cause of action, and that a general release for valuable consideration (or even, in some cases, for none), is a satisfaction of the injury and a release of the cause of action . . .

In some cases, it was even held that a release of one jointly liable acted as a release of all, even though the release contained an express provision to the contrary.

The injustice of the traditional rule was that it frequently acted to extinguish a cause of action which was only partly compensated, even though the parties themselves had no such intention. The rule also made it very difficult for a claimant to settle a claim by partial settlements with several persons who were jointly liable for his injury. A major cause of these difficulties was the doctrine of joint liability itself, a doctrine largely grounded in a policy of assuring compensation for injured plaintiffs, but which the traditional rule paradoxically converted into a burden and a trap for unwary plaintiffs . . . In recent years, the strict limitations of the traditional rule have been largely abandoned . . .

[Recent cases] have established a clear distinction in Ohio law between releases and covenants not to sue. In the case of a release that is unqualified and absolute in its terms, a presumption arises that the injury has been fully satisfied. This presumption may be rebutted by the express reservation of rights against other parties or the release may be avoided under the powers of equity, where the releasor can establish by clear and convincing evidence that it was executed by mutual mistake.

A covenant not to sue, which does not purport to release or transfer any cause of action for an injury and which does not expressly recognize the consideration paid thereunder as full satisfaction for the injury, will not bar action against others for causing the injury where the injury has not been fully compensated. Such a covenant need not expressly reserve rights against others . . .

The distinctions between these two types of instruments doubtless have been relied upon by claimants and the meaning of those distinctions should be clear to practitioners of Ohio law. A party is free to bargain for the type of instrument he desires to execute and for the consideration due thereunder. His legal rights and liabilities may well depend upon the form of instrument chosen, particularly in cases where there is a right of indemnity or a contractual right of contribution, or where some group of individuals are all subject to possible liability for a single injury. One charged as a tortfeasor may well wish to protect himself against claims of other tortfeasors or to avoid involvement as a witness in further litigation. An absolute unqualified release in full satisfaction of an injury in such cases gives the party released the protection he would not obtain under a covenant not to sue, and these benefits may well be reflected in the consideration given for the release.

In the instant case, plaintiff, with advice of counsel, chose to execute an unconditional release for reconsideration of $6,000, over three and one-half years after the original injury. Such a release is presumed in law to be a release for the benefit of all the wrongdoers who might also be liable, and to be a satisfaction of the injury. The presumption stands unrebutted in the instant case, and bars suit to recover for an alleged aggravation of injuries.

For the foregoing reasons, the judgment of the Court of Appeals is affirmed.

o **Recap of the Case.** Frequently, there is more than one potential or actual defendant to a law suit. It is not unusual for one or more of these defendants to express a willingness to settle the case against them. The question raised by this case is: Will a general release which does not specifically reserve the right of the plaintiff to sue other defendants relieve all defendants of liability? The answer, at least in this jurisdiction, is "yes."

PRACTITIONER LOSES COUNTERSUIT FOR MALICIOUS PROSECUTION AND PATIENT NOT LIABLE

In recent years, physicians have attempted to discourage malpractice suits by filing counterclaims against patients and attorneys who brought suit without just cause. These suits have been based upon claims of abuse of process, malicious prosecution, intentional infliction of emotional distress, defamation, and negligence. More recently, such suits have been based upon a form of action called *prima facie tort*. *Prima facie tort* is "the intentional malicious injury to another by otherwise lawful means without economic or social justification, but solely to harm the other." Countersuits based on these theories produce mixed results at best, as evidenced by *Martin v. Trevino*, 578 S.W.2d 763 (Tex.Civ.App. 1978) and *Butler v. Morgan*, 590 S.W.2d 543 (Tex.Civ.App. 1979). In both of these cases, the courts ruled against both defendants primarily because they could not show special damages, i.e., a specific injury to their person or property as a result of plaintiff's malpractice suit.

Martin v. Trevino, 578 S.W. 2d 763 (Tex.Civ.App.1978) Texas Court of Appeals

. . . Attorney J. Manuel Banales filed suit on behalf of his client, plaintiff Trevino, against defendant Dr. Martin for medical malpractice. Dr. Martin filed a general denial and a counterclaim against Mrs. Trevino and a third–party action against Attorney Banales and his law firm, Huerta, Pena,

Beckman, Rodriguez & Alfaro (hereinafter "attorneys") alleging, in substance, that plaintiff Trevino and her attorneys negligently filed the medical malpractice suit without just cause and without proper investigation to determine whether or not such suit could be legally or factually justified. Dr. Martin alleged that the filing of the medical malpractice suit resulted in "actual expenses and damages" and that "he had lost, and will in all reasonable probability lose in the future, revenue from his medical practice because of such unfounded claims and assertions against him . . .

In order to maintain an action for malicious prosecution in Texas, a party must plead and prove that: 1) a civil judicial proceeding was previously filed; 2) the defendant in the malicious prosecution case caused the original suit to be filed; 3) the commencement of the original proceeding was malicious; 4) no probable cause existed for the filing of the original proceeding; 5) termination of the original suit in favor of the party prosecuting the later malicious prosecution action, and 6) damages conforming to the legal standards under Texas law . . . The gravamen of an action for malicious prosecution is improperly making a party the subject of legal process to his detriment. Texas adheres to the rule that an award of damages for prosecution of civil suits with malice and without probable cause cannot be recovered unless the party sued, suffers some interference, by reason of the suit, with his person or property . . . . A pleading which does not allege some interference with the complainant's person or property fails to state a cause of action for malicious prosecution and is fatally defective . . .

The primary dispute between the parties concerning Dr. Martin's alleged cause of action for malicious prosecution is whether or not Dr. Martin has pled special damages (interference with his person or property) as required by Texas law. Dr. Martin admits that his damages consist only of actual litigation expenses and "professional defamatory–type" damages. Dr. Martin argues, however, that the special damage rule is outmoded in today's society where the number of groundless medical malpractice suits is increasing at an alarming rate. He also contends that there is no empirical support to justify the conclusion that the special damage requirement is necessary in order to avoid a chilling effect on good faith litigation. He contends that it is unlikely that the adoption of the opposite rule would result in endless counterlitigation and counter–counterliti– gation. Finally, Dr. Martin argues that the injustice inherent in the special damage requirement is particularly apparent when groundless malpractice suits are brought against physicians because the physician's professional reputation is unnecessarily damaged. This harm, Dr. Martin contends, is damage special to the physician and should be so recognized by this Court.

In support of Dr. Martin's argument that this Court should either abolish the special damage requirement or conclude that harm to a doctor's professional reputation and medical practice amounts to special damages, the Malpractice Defense Committee, *Amicus Curiae*, states that Texas courts have already broadened the concept of special damages in bankruptcy and lunacy proceedings . . .

. . . It has long been the law in Texas that a suit for damages for malicious prosecution will not lie "unless the party sued suffers some interference by [the] reason of the [original suit against him], with his person or property." This rule was followed in each of the cases cited by the Malpractice Defense Committee.

. . . Here Dr. Martin did not allege that the original malpractice suit interfered in any way with his person or property. The special damage rule was initially adopted by our Supreme Court for policy reasons to assure every potential litigant free and open access to the judicial system without fear of a countersuit for malicious prosecution . . .

We are of the opinion that the general policy reasons for adopting the special damage rule in Texas remain viable today. If special damages result, the defendant has his remedy. The special damage requirement also prevents successful defendants in the initial proceedings from using their favorable judgment as a reason to institute a new suit based on malicious prosecution, resulting in needless and endless vexatious lawsuits. Furthermore, it is not the duty of this Court to gather and to interpret empirical data for the purpose of determining whether or not the special damage rule should be abolished. This is a legislative task which has already been undertaken in part by the 65th Texas Legislature . . .

. . . Dr. Martin contends that his pleadings alleged a viable cause of action based upon abuse of process. Appellees contend that Dr. Martin failed to allege any abuse or misuse of process after its original issuance and, therefore, failed to plead a viable cause of action for abuse of process . . .

In order for a person to recover for abuse of process, he must plead and prove three essential elements: 1) that the defendant made an illegal, improper, or perverted use of the process, a use neither warranted nor authorized by the process;

2) that the defendant had an ulterior motive or purpose in exercising such illegal, perverted or improper use of the process; and 3) that damage resulted to the plaintiff as a result of such irregular act . . .

In this case, Dr. Martin alleged that " . . . the Plaintiff improperly procured the issuance of the citation . . ." The mere procurement or issuance with a malicious intent or without probable cause is not actionable. This is so because there must be an improper use of the process after its issuance . . . Texas has generally recognized a cause of action for abuse of process in situations where the original process, such as a writ of garnishment or writ of sequestration, has been abused to accomplish an end other than that which the writ was designed to accomplish.

Dr. Martin argues that his allegations, in effect, state that "Mrs. Trevino and her attorneys secured the issuance of citation in the malpractice case, not because of a good faith belief in the possible merit of the suit, but only in an attempt to do harm to Dr. Martin (e.g., trying to profit at his expense by coercing a settlement)." Dr. Martin's pleadings, however, do not suggest that Mrs. Trevino or her attorneys actually did attempt to coerce a settlement. Even if we assume that the original medical malpractice action was maliciously instituted, Dr. Martin's allegations are fatally defective because they fail to allege an improper use of the process other than the mere institution of the civil action. There were no damages other than that necessarily incident to filing a lawsuit . . .

. . . Dr. Martin contends that his pleadings state a valid cause of action for damages against Mrs. Trevino's attorneys for breach of their professional responsibilities. Dr. Martin's supplemental cross pleadings allege that the professional responsibilities imposed on all attorneys under Texas law prohibit attorneys from filing frivolous suits. Dr. Martin further alleged that Mrs. Trevino's attorneys filed the original medical malpractice suit against him "without proper investigation" and "without an informed basis of determining prior to the filing of such suit that such suit had reasonable merit."

. . . [A]ll persons who practice law in the State of Texas are members of the State Bar and are subject to the provisions of the State Bar Act and the rules adopted by the Supreme Court of Texas . . .

. . . Dr. Martin relies on Disciplinary Rule-7-102(A) which provides in relevant part:

(A) In his representations of a client, a lawyer shall not: (1) [f]ile a suit, assert a position, . . . or take other action on behalf of his client when he knows or when it is obvious that such action would serve merely to harass or maliciously injure another. (2) Knowingly advance a claim that is unwarranted under existing law, except that he may advance such claim . . . if it can be supported by good faith argument for an extension, modification, or reversal of existing law.

Dr. Martin argues that a cause of action based upon the breach of professional responsibility standards should be available against attorneys filing unjustified medical malpractice suits because [b] "the public, including Dr. Martin, should be entitled to professional accountability by the Bar in this regard." Regardless of the arguable merit of such a contention, Dr. Martin's point . . . must be overruled because the violation by an attorney of the disciplinary rules adopted by the Texas Supreme Court does not of itself create a private cause of action.

Assuming, as we must, that Dr. Martin could prove that Mrs. Trevino's attorneys had violated Disciplinary Rule 7–102(A), Martin failed to file a grievance under procedures enumerated in the State Bar Rules adopted by the Supreme Court for the redress of alleged professional misconduct. The sole remedial method for a violation of the Code is the imposition of disciplinary measures after a hearing by the District Grievance Committee which is authorized to "receive complaints of professional misconduct" and "make such investigation of each complaint . . . [prior] to taking action . . . The remedy provided pursuant to these sections for the professional misconduct of an attorney is a public one, not a private one . . .

In point of error 3D, Dr. Martin contends that the trial court's summary judgment was erroneous because his pleadings stated a viable cause of action based upon negligence. In the counterpleading Dr. Martin filed before plaintiff Trevino's medical malpractice claim was non–suited, Dr. Martin alleged a negligence–type cause of action against both Mrs. Trevino and her attorneys, in essence as follows: 1) that plaintiff Trevino's attorneys acted as Trevino's agent and legal representative so that the consequences of their actions are imputable to her and she is legally responsible to Dr. Martin for their acts; 2) that the attorneys filed the medical malpractice suit in question when, in fact, no justification thereof existed, and without proper investigation prior to the filing of such suit; 3) that the attorneys were aware that the filing of an unjustified medical malpractice suit would be damaging to Dr. Martin's reputation and would directly and proximately cause him to incur additional expense and to suffer loss of revenue from his medical practice; 4) that the attorneys were also aware that medical malpractice suits are frequently marginal and detrimental unless proper investigation is made prior to the time the suit is instituted; 5) that the attorneys made no investigation and did not determine prior to the filing of the suit whether or not there was any proper justification; 6) that the defendant attorneys did in fact legally owe Dr. Martin the duty of investigating the claim they proposed to file and their failure to do so constituted negligent conduct which resulted in damage to Dr. Martin and that such negligence is imputable to plaintiff Trevino; 7) that Dr. Martin incurred actual expenses and damages of at least $5,000.00 and that he had lost $25,000.00 in revenue from his medical practice because of such unfounded claims asserted by Mrs. Trevino's attorneys; and 8) that Mrs. Trevino's attorneys acted wantonly and with malice aforethought so that Dr. Martin should be entitled to recover exemplary damages of at least $25,000.00.

Dr. Martin asserts that the controlling question presented to this Court is whether or not, under Texas law, an attorney has the duty to investigate a claim he proposes to file and to determine whether or not the suit is justified prior to the time the actual cause is filed. Dr. Martin asserts that "[t]his is a case of first impression in Texas on this particular point with respect to counterlitigation by a professional person, such as a physician, who has been damaged by the mere filing of an unjustified defamatory–type malpractice suit."

Other courts in Texas have considered the general issue of whether or not an attorney should be held liable in negligence to a party other than his client for damages resulting from the performance of the attorney's services. . . These cases have generally concluded that an attorney is exempt from liability to a party other than his client for damages resulting in the performance of service which engages and requires the office or the professional training, skill, and authority of an attorney because an attorney deals at arm's length with adverse parties, and that he is not liable to such adverse parties for his actions, as an attorney on behalf of his client. The primary duty the attorney owes is to his client so long as it is compatible with his professional responsibility. If he violates this responsibility, the remedy is public, not private . . .

Our review of Texas authorities and the approach taken in other jurisdictions leads us to the conclusion that this is not the proper case to abolish the privity requirement. Dr. Martin stands in a pure adversary relationship with plaintiff Trevino and her attorneys. The doctor is not an intended beneficiary of the attorney's services. This view is consistent with virtually every other case which has considered the negligence theory in cases such as this where the physician believes he has been sued for medical malpractice without just cause . . .

In point of error 3E, Dr. Martin, in effect, requests this Court to recognize a nameless tort concept, adopted and known by some jurisdictions, as "Prima Facie Tort". Dr. Martin contends that his counterpleadings stated a valid cause of action because he alleged: "The actions of the Plaintiff and her attorneys in this lawsuit amounted to a 'Prima Facie Tort', which included the infliction of intentional harm, resulting in damage, without excuse or justification, resulting from unjustified, intentional, and malicious actions on the part of the Plaintiff and her attorneys, which produced and proximately caused the damages set forth in the Defendant's Counter Claim."

Prima Facie Tort can be defined as: the infliction of an intentional harm without excuse or justification by an act or series of acts which results in special damage. It does not fall within the categories of traditional torts . . . The basic elements of the Prima Facie Tort cause of action that are apparently emerging include: 1) an intent to injure on the part of the defendant; 2) a lack of justification in so acting; and 3) special damages, alleged with particularity. Generally, an allegation that the physician has sustained damage to his professional standing and reputation is not sufficient.

. . . If we were to adopt the Prima Facie Tort concept in this case, the effect would be to circumvent the special damages required in malicious prosecution actions and most Prima Facie Tort cases, and the privity requirement of negligence actions brought against an attorney by a third party not in privity with the attorney's client. This we will not do. Furthermore, our adoption of the Prima Facie Tort concept in this cause would preempt the Legislature's adoption of the Medical Liability and Insurance Improvement Act and its provisions regarding the institution of bad faith medical care claims. If this particular type of a cause of action has merit, it should be mandated by the Legislature as a matter of public policy, and not by our courts. Dr. Martin's point of error 3E is overruled . . .

Butler v. Morgan, 590 S.W. 2d 543 (Tex.Civ.App.1979)
Texas Court of Appeals

. . . Mary Morgan filed a medical malpractice suit against Doctor Donald B. Butler, and others, which proceeded to trial and resulted in a judgment in favor of all of the defendants. Thereafter, Doctor Butler filed this suit for damages asserting a cause of action based on malicious prosecution . . .

It is well established that one of the essential elements which must be pleaded and proved for recovery based on malicious prosecution is that the plaintiff has suffered damages conforming to legal standards under Texas law.

The plaintiff alleged that he suffered injury to his personal and professional reputation as a surgeon and physician, personal humiliation, mental anguish and distress. He asserted that he had been damaged in his practice of medicine, which depends largely upon referrals from other physicians, and that he was forced to neglect his professional practice to his damage. He asserted that his professional malpractice insurance had been cancelled as a result of this malpractice suit and that his insurance premiums had been increased, caused at least in part by the filing of this suit.

The rule is firmly established in Texas which denies an award of damages for the prosecution of civil suits, with malice and without probable cause, unless the party sued suffers some interference, by reason of the suit, with his person or property . . .

The mere filing of a civil suit resulting in damage to the defendant is not such an interference with the person or property of the defendant in the suit as will support an action for malicious prosecution. The damage which the plaintiff has alleged he suffered flowed, directly or indirectly, from the fact that the suit was filed.

The judgment is affirmed.

o **Recap of the Cases.** The "malpractice crisis" encouraged practitioners to protect themselves from malpractice suits to the greatest possible extent. As a result, practitioners sued by patients began suing the patients in return. In order to win on a claim for malicious prosecution, the most common basis for this type of suit, the practitioner must be able to prove special damages. As the court explained in these two cases, damage to the practitioner's reputation and practice are not special damages. In order to prove special damages and win a malpractice case, practitioners must be able to show damage to their person or property. Since the practitioners in these two cases could not prove special damages, they lost their cases against patients.

INTENTIONAL TORTS

7

Assault and Battery

Assault and battery are actually two separate torts. An assault is conduct which creates a reasonable apprehension of being touched in an injurious manner. A battery is an actual touching.

PATIENT RECOVERS DAMAGES FOR ASSAULT BY PRACTITIONER

The simplest form of assault and battery within the practice setting occurs when practitioners strike patients. In *Burton v. Leftwich*, 123 So.2d 766 (La.Ct.App. 1960), for example, the plaintiff took her young child to the defendant's office for removal of stitches. During the procedure, the child became upset and had difficulty remaining still. The defendant struck the child several times on the thigh. The bruises from these blows were visible for several weeks after this incident. Plaintiff was awarded damages for assault and battery.

Burton v. Leftwich, 123 So.2d 766 (La.Ct.App. 1960)
Louisiana Court of Appeals

. . .During September, 1957, the defendant, Dr. James W. Leftwich, treated Pamela for a laceration of the toe, which required suturing. In obedience to his instructions, the child was returned later to the doctor's office for the purpose of removing the sutures. At the time, the child was accompanied by her mother and a neighbor. It was suggested by Dr. Leftwich that the child should lie prone while the sutures were being removed and Mrs. Burton was instructed to help hold the child in a prone position. Pamela began to cry and make repeated efforts to sit up, all of which apparently interfered with the task confronting the doctor, and the latter administered several blows with his open hand to the child's right thigh in order to require her to be still. The mother was incensed at this and immediately took the child out of the doctor's office and later that same day the sutures were removed without incident at the office of another doctor. The evidence established beyond peradventure that the blows inflicted by the defendant caused bruises which remained visible for a period of as much as three weeks.

The position of the defendant is that he acted pursuant to his professional judgment that such steps were necessary to the maintenance of discipline and that the course of action so taken was preferable to a scissors puncture which might have resulted from the child's continued leg movement.

We agree with the judge a quo in his assigned reasons that the defendant used exceedingly bad judgment in striking the child and liability has been established.

Counsel for appellant argues that the award of $500 as made by the trial court was excessive and in fact, the injuries sustained by the child were of such a minor nature that they were not sufficient to justify an award of damages, thus invoking the doctrine of de minimis lex non curat. On this appeal consideration may not be given to the claims of Mrs. Burton, who sought damages for mental anguish occasioned to her by the sight of her child being unlawfully struck, forasmuch as no appeal on her behalf was taken. In behalf of the appellee it is argued that the effect of the chastisement was to heighten the child's psychological apprehension of medical treatment. This contention is not sufficiently established as a basis for the award of damages. Later during the day the sutures were removed by another doctor without great difficulty. This fact seems to indicate the child suffered no extreme emotional upset.

We cannot agree with appellant that the injuries were insufficient to justify an award of damages, but we are of the opinion that as there is no evidence the chastisement caused the child enduring or severe pain, and as the injury complained of was not of such nature as to require medical treatment, such damages should be nominal . . .

The judgment from which appealed is amended by reducing the award in favor of the appellees from $500 to $250, and as so amended, the judgment is affirmed . . .

o **Recap of the Case.** The practical application of this case to nursing practice shows that nurses are rarely able to apply force to patients without incurring liability. Every other possible means for dealing with the patient must be attempted first.

PLAINTIFF NOT AWARDED DAMAGES IN ASSAULT BY PRACTITIONER

The court in *Mattochs v. Bell*, 194 A.2d 307 (D.C. 1963) decided that even though the defendant struck a child, he was not liable for assault and battery. In this case, the child bit the defendant, and the defendant slapped the child to encourage the child to loosen her grip on defendant's finger.

Mattochs v. Bell, 194 A.2d 307 (D.C. 1963) District of Columbia Court of Appeals

This case presents a rather unusual factual situation. The plaintiff is a female child who was twenty-three months old at the time in question. The defendant is a medical student who at the time was serving as an extern in the emergency room of District of Columbia General Hospital. The child was taken to the hospital by her mother for treatment of a lacerated tongue. As defendant attempted to examine the child's mouth she clamped her teeth on defendant's left middle finger and bit hard enough to cause blood to spurt from the finger, although it was enclosed in a rubber glove. Defendant shouted to the child to open her mouth but she retained her grip on the finger. He twice unsuccessfully attempted to extricate his finger by forcing a tongue depressor into her mouth. He then slapped the child on the cheek with his hand and this caused her to open her mouth and release the finger. A doctor who immediately treated the finger testified that "the wound was deep enough to have touched the bone." The foregoing facts were not disputed but there was a conflict of testimony regarding the severity of the slap.

The child through its mother brought this action against defendant for damages for assault and battery. The trial court denied recovery, finding that although the action of defendant may have been rash it was not malicious, that the blow was not severe and that the child was not injured.

On this appeal it is urged that when it was established that defendant intentionally slapped the child, and assault and battery was proved, that this proof entitled the child to a recovery unless justification was established, and that there was no evidence from which the court could have found a justification.

. . . Here we have one slap that was not "hard" instead of several severe slaps; here we have "poor or hasty judgment" instead of exceeding bad judgment; and here we have an emergency situation which did not exist in the other. In the other case the slaps were in the nature of discipline. Here the single slap was more in the nature of a protective or defensive measure.

. . . [F]rom what little authority there is available, it would appear that whether pecuniary liability is imposed on a doctor (or hospital based on respondeat superior), because of the action taken by him to restrain or discipline a patient, depends on whether the situation called for the use of force, and if so, whether the amount of force used and the manner in which it was applied were proper under the circumstances. We think the rule stated is sound and, applying it to the situation before us, hold that the trial court could properly find that force was required, that it was not applied in an improper manner and that a recovery should be denied.

Affirmed.

o **Recap of the Case.** Based upon the *Mattochs* case, nurses may conclude that there are circumstances in which the use of force on patients is justified. If the situation calls for the use of force because it is an emergency, i.e., all other means for dealing with the patient have been exhausted, nurses may not be liable. Nurses must be careful, however, to apply only an appropriate amount of support and apply it in a proper manner. The key to avoiding liability is the exercise of good judgment, taking into account all of the circumstances of a particular event.

PRACTITIONER WHO PERFORMS OPERATION WITHOUT PATIENT'S CONSENT COMMITS AN ASSAULT

In more complex situations, an assault and battery occurs when a practitioner renders treatment without consent from the patient. In *Schloendorff v. Society of N.Y. Hospital*, 211 N.Y. 125, 105 N.E. 92 (1914), the court held that a practitioner committed a battery when he removed a tumor after the patient consented to an examination only. Practitioners may also commit a battery when they obtain permission for treatment, but go beyond the scope of the permission to render treatment to which the patient did not consent. A battery also occurs when practitioners obtain permission for treatment, but because the practitioner does not thoroughly explain the risks to the patient, the consent to treatment is invalid.

Schloendorff v. Society of N.Y. Hospital
211 N.Y. 125, 105 N.E. 92 (1914) New York Court of Appeals

To this hospital the plaintiff came in January, 1908. She was suffering from some disorder of the stomach. She asked the superintendent or one of his assistants what the charge would be, and was told that it would be $7 a week. She became an inmate of the hospital, and after some weeks of treatment, the house physician, Dr. Bartlett, discovered a lump, which proved to a fibroid tumor. He consulted the visiting physician, Dr. Stimson, who advised an operation. The plaintiff's testimony is that the character of the lump could not, so the physicians informed her, be determined without an ether examination. She consented to such an examination, but notified Dr. Bartlett, as she says, that there must be no operation. She was taken at night from the medical to the surgical ward and prepared for an operation by a nurse. On the following day ether was administered, and, while she was unconscious, a tumor was removed. Her testimony is that this was done without her consent or knowledge. She is contradicted both by Dr. Stimson and by Dr. Bartlett, as well as by many of the attendant nurses. For the purpose of this appeal, however, since a verdict was directed in favor of the defendant, her narrative, even if improbable, must be taken as true. Following the operation, and, according to the testimony of her witnesses, because of it, gangrene developed in her left arm, some of her fingers had to be amputated, and her sufferings were intense. She now seeks to charge the hospital with liability for the wrong . . .

In the case at hand, the wrong complained of is not merely negligence. It is trespass. Every human being of adult years and sound mind has a right to determine what shall be done with his own body; and a surgeon who performs an operation without his patient's consent commits an assault, for which he is liable in damage.

. . . This is true, except in cases of emergency where the patient is unconscious, and where it is necessary to operate before consent can be obtained. The fact that the wrong complained of here is trespass, rather than negligence, distinguishes the case from most of the cases that have preceded it. In such circumstances the hospital's exemption from liability can hardly rest upon implied waiver. Relatively to this transaction, the plaintiff was a stranger. She had never consented to become a patient for any purpose other than an examination under ether. She had never waived the right to recover damages for any wrong resulting from this operation, for she had forbidden the operation.

. . . I do not think that anything said by the plaintiff to any of the defendant's nurses fairly gave notice to them that the purpose was to cut open the plaintiff's body without her consent. The visiting surgeon in charge of the case was one of the most eminent in the city of New York. The assistant physicians and surgeons were men of tested merit. The plaintiff was prepared for the operation at night. She said to the night nurse, according to her statement, that she was not going to be operated on, that she was merely going to be examined under ether, and the nurse professed to understand that this was so. "Every now and then I asked: 'Do you understand that I am not to be operated on?' "Yes; I understand; ether examination.' 'But,' I asked, 'I understand that this preparation is for operation.' She said: 'It is just the same in ether examination as in operation—the same preparation.'"
The nurse with whom this conversation is said to have occurred left the ward early in the morning, and the operation was performed in her absence the following afternoon. Was she to infer from the plaintiff's words that a distinguished surgeon intended to mutilate the plaintiff's body in defiance of the plaintiff's orders? Was it her duty, as a result of this talk, to report to the superintendent of the hospital that the ward was about to be utilized for the commission of an assault? I think that no such interpretation of the facts would have suggested itself to any reasonable mind. The preparation for an ether

examination is to some extent the same as for an operation. The hour was midnight, and the plaintiff was nervous and excited. The nurse soothed her by acquiescing in the statement that an ether examination was all that was intended, and how soon the operation was to follow, if at all, the nurse had no means of knowing. Still less had she reason to suspect that it would follow against the plaintiff's orders. If, when the following afternoon came, the plaintiff persisted in being unwilling to submit to an operation, the presumption was then that the distinguished surgeon in charge of the case would perform none. There may be cases where a patient ought not to be advised of a contemplated operation until shortly before the appointed hour. To discuss such a subject at midnight might cause needless and even harmful agitation. About such matters a nurse is not qualified to judge. She is drilled to habits of strict obedience. She is accustomed to rely unquestioningly upon the judgment of her superiors. No woman occupying such a position would reasonably infer from the plaintiff's words that it was the purpose of the surgeons to operate whether the plaintiff, forbade it or not . . .

Still more clearly the defendant is not chargeable with notice because of the plaintiff's statements to the physician who administered the gas and ether. She says she asked him whether an operation was to be performed, and that he told her he did not know; that his duty was to give the gas, and nothing more. She answered that she wished to tell some one that there must be no operation, that she had come merely for an ether examination, and he told her that, if she had come only for examination, nothing else would be done. There is nothing in the record to suggest that he believed anything to the contrary. He took no part in the operation, and had no knowledge of it. After the gas was administered, she was taken into another room. It does not appear, therefore, that this physician was a party to any wrong. In any event, he was not the servant of the hospital. His position in that respect does not differ from that of the operating surgeon. If he was a party to the trespass he did not subject the defendant to liability . . .

The judgment should be affirmed, with costs.

o **Recap of the Case.** The practical lesson of this case is that practitioners, including nurses, are liable for treatment rendered which is not authorized by patients. Nurses should not be misled by the fact that in this situation, the nurse was not liable for unauthorized surgery. The principles described in the case are applicable to all types of treatment. Nurses are held liable for unauthorized treatment rendered by them.

DAMAGES AWARDED FOR ASSAULT AND BATTERY LIMITED BY BENEFICIAL RESULTS OF SURGERY AND GOOD FAITH OF PRACTITIONER

In *Mohr v. Williams*, 95 Minn. 261, 104 N.W.12 (1905), the plaintiff consented to surgery on her right ear. After she received anesthesia and became unconscious, defendant carefully examined her left ear and determined that it required surgery instead of the right ear. The defendant then skillfully performed surgery on plaintiff's right ear.

The patient later sued, claiming that the defendant committed an assault and battery. The defendant argued that the plaintiff's circumstances amounted to an emergency so that consent was not required from the plaintiff. The defendant also argued that the plaintiff's consent to the same type of surgery on her right ear should be applicable for surgery on her left ear. All of the defendant's arguments were rejected by the court, and the court affirmed that the defendant was liable for assault and battery. The court noted, however, that the defendant's good faith and the lack of injury to the plaintiff should be taken into account to decide the amount of damages awarded to the plaintiff, or if she in fact should receive any damages at all.

Mohr v. Williams, 95 Minn. 261, 104 N.W.12 (1905)
Supreme Court of Minnesota

Defendant is a physician and surgeon of standing and character, making an extensive practice in the city of St. Paul. He was consulted by plaintiff, who complained to him of trouble with her right ear, and, at her request, made an examination of that organ for the purpose of ascertaining its condition. He also at the same time examined her left ear, but, owing to foreign substances therein, was unable to make a full and complete diagnosis at that time. The examination of her right ear disclosed a large perforation in the lower portion of the drum membrane, and a large polyp in the middle ear, which indicated that some of the small bones of the middle ear (ossicles) were probably diseased. He informed plaintiff of the result of his examination, and advised an operation for the purpose of removing the polyp and diseased ossicles. After consultation with her family physician, and one or two further consultations with defendant, plaintiff decided to submit to the proposed operation. She was not informed that her left ear was in any way diseased, and understood that the necessity for an operation applied to her right ear only. She repaired to the hospital, and was placed under the influence of anesthetics; and, after being made unconscious, defendant made a thorough examination of her left ear, and found it in a more serious condition than her right one. A small perforation was discovered high up in the drum membrane, hooded, and with granulated edges, and the bone of the inner wall of the middle ear was diseased and dead. He called this discovery to the attention of Dr. Davis—plaintiff's family physician, who attended the operation at her request—who also examined the ear, and confirmed defendant in his diagnosis. Defendant also further examined the right ear, and found its condition less serious than expected, and finally concluded that the left, instead of the right, should be operated upon; devoting to the right ear other treatment. He then performed the operation of ossiculectomy on plaintiff's left ear; removing a portion of the drum membrane, and scraping away the diseased portion of the inner wall of the ear. The operation was in every way successful and skillfully performed. It is claimed by plaintiff that the operation greatly impaired her hearing, seriously injured her person, and not having been consented to by her, was wrongful and unlawful, constituting an assault and battery; and she brought this action to recover damages therefor . . .

It is contended that final judgment should be ordered in [the physician's] favor for the following reasons: (a) That it appears from the evidence received on the trial that plaintiff consented to the operation on her left ear. (b) If the court shall find that no such consent was given, that, under the circumstances disclosed by the record, no consent was necessary. (c) That, under the facts disclosed, an action for assault and battery will not lie; it appearing conclusively, as counsel urge, that there is a total lack of evidence showing or tending to show malice or an evil intent on the part of defendant, or that the operation was negligently performed.

We shall consider first the question whether, under the circumstances shown in the record, the consent of plaintiff to the operation was necessary. If, under the particular facts of this case, such consent was unnecessary, no recovery can be had, for the evidence fairly shows that the operation complained of was skillfully performed and of a generally beneficial nature. But if the consent of plaintiff was necessary, then the further questions presented become important . . . We have given it very deliberate consideration, and are unable to concur with counsel for defendant in their contention that the consent of plaintiff was unnecessary. The evidence tends to show that, upon the first examination of plaintiff, defendant pronounced the left ear in good condition, and that, at the time plaintiff repaired to the hospital to submit to the operation on her right ear, she was under the impression that no difficulty existed as to the left. In fact, she testified that she had not previously experienced any trouble with that organ. It cannot be doubted that ordinarily the patient must be consulted, and his consent given, before a physician may operate upon him . . . There is logic in the principle thus stated, for, in all other trades, professions, or occupations, contracts are entered into by the mutual agreement of the interested parties, and are required to be performed in accordance with their letter and spirit. No reason occurs to us why the same rule should not apply between physician and patient. If the physician advises his patient to submit to a particular operation, and the patient weighs the dangers and risks incident to its performance, and finally consents, he thereby, in effect, enters into a contract authorizing his physician to operate to the extent of the consent given, but no further. It is not, however, contended by defendant that under ordinary circumstances consent is unnecessary, but that, under the particular circumstances of this case, consent was implied; that it was an emergency case, such as to authorize the operation without express consent or permission. The medical profession has made signal progress in solving the problems of health and disease, and they may justly point with pride to the advancements made in supplementing nature and correcting deformities, and relieving pain and suffering. The physician impliedly contracts that he possesses, and will exercise in the treatment of patients, skill and learning, and that he will exercise reasonable care and exert his best judgment to bring about favorable results. The methods of treatment are committed almost exlusively to his judgment, but we are aware of no rule or principle of law which would extend to him free license respecting surgical operations. Reasonable latitude must, however, be allowed the physician in a particular case; and we would not lay down any rule which would unreasonably interfere with the exercise of his discretion, or prevent him from taking such measures as his judgment dictated for the welfare of the patient in a case of emergency. If a person should be injured to the extent of rendering him unconscious, and his injuries were of such a nature as to require prompt surgical attention, a physician called to attend him would be justified in applying such medical or surgical treatment as might be necessary for the preservation of his life or limb, and consent on the part of the injured person would be implied. And again, if, in the course of an operation to which the patient consented, the physician should discover conditions not anitcipated before the operation was commenced, and which, if not removed, would endanger the life or health of the patient, he would, though no express consent was obtained or given, be justified in extending the operation to remove and overcome them. But such is not the case at bar. The diseased condition of plaintiff's left ear was not discovered in the course of an operation on the right, which was authorized, but upon an independent examination of that organ, made after the authorized operation was found unnecessary. Nor is the evidence such as to justify the court in holding, as a matter of law, that it was such an affection as would result immediately in the serious injury of plaintiff, or such an emergency as to justify proceeding without her consent. She had experienced no particular difficulty with that ear, and the questions as to when its diseased condition would become alarming or fatal, and whether there was an immediate necessity for an operation, were, under the evidence, questions of fact for the jury.

The contention of defendant that the operation was consented to by plaintiff is not sustained by the evidence . . . This contention is based upon the fact that she was represented on the occasion in question by her family physician; that the condition of her left ear was made known to him, and the propriety of an operation thereon suggested, to which he made no objection. It is urged that by his conduct he assented to it, and that plaintiff was bound thereby. It is not claimed that he gave his express consent. It is not disputed by that the family physician of plaintiff was present on the occasion of the operation, and at her request. But the purpose of his presence was not that he might participate in the operation, nor does it appear that he was authorized to consent to any change in the one originally proposed to be made. Plaintiff was naturally nervous and fearful of the consequences of being placed under the influence of anesthestics, and the presence of her family physician was requested under the impression that it would allay and calm her fears . . .

The last contention of defendant is that the act complained of did not amount to an assault and battery. This is based upon the theory that, as plaintiff's left ear was in fact diseased, in a condition dangerous and threatening to her health, the operation was necessary, and, having been skillfully performed at a time when plaintiff had requested a like operation on the other ear, the charge of assault and battery cannot be sustained; that, in view of these conditions, and the claim that there was no negligence on the part of defendant, and an entire absence of any evidence tending to show an evil intent, the court should say, as a matter of law, that no assault and battery was committed, even though she did not consent to the operation. In other words, that the absence of a showing that defendant was actuated by a wrongful intent, or guilty of negligence, relieves the act of defendant from the charge of an unlawful assault and battery. We are unable to reach that conclusion, though the contention is not without merit. It would seem to follow from what has been said on the other features of the case that the act of defendant amounted at least to a technical assault and battery. If the operation was performed without plaintiff's consent, and the circumstances were not such as to justify its performance without, it was wrongful; and if it was wrongful, it was unlawful. [E]very person has a right to complete immunity of his person from physical interference of others, except in so far as contact may be necessary under the general doctrine of privilege; and any unlawful or unauthorized touching of the person of another, except it be in the spirit of pleasantry, constitutes an assault and battery. In the case at bar, as we have already seen, the question whether defendant's act in performing the operation upon plaintiff was authorized was a question for the jury to determine. If it was unauthorized, then it was, within what we have said, unlawful. It was a violent assault, not a mere pleasantry; and even though no negligence is shown, it was wrongful and unlawful.

The amount of plaintiff's recovery, if she is entitled to recover at all, must depend upon the character and extent of the injury inflicted upon her, in determining which the nature of the malady intended to be healed and the beneficial nature of the operation should be taken into consideration, as well as the good faith of the defendant.

Order affirmed.

o **Recap of the Case.** Many practitioners conclude that the law is applied with careful adherence to all of its technicalities regardless of result. The *Mohr* case is an example of a court's overriding concern with a fair result. The practitioner in this case technically committed an assault and battery. The court, however, noted that the unauthorized surgery was done skillfully and did not harm the patient. Consequently, the amount of money given to the patient will be small, if she receives any at all.

8

False Imprisonment

Practitioners are liable for false imprisonment when they unlawfully restrain the movement of their patients. This tort is frequently applicable to involuntary commitments to mental health facilities.

INSTITUTIONAL OFFICIALS NOT LIABLE FOR FALSE IMPRISONMENT

For example, in *Maniaci v. Marquette University*, 50 Wis.2d 287, 1984 N.W.2d 168 (1971), university officials committed a student to a mental institution in order to stop her from leaving school. The court decided that the officials had not falsely imprisoned the plaintiff because she was committed to the institution in a completely lawful manner. The results of this case are applicable to nurses. Practitioners may, for example, be liable for false imprisonment if they unnecessarily apply restraints to patients. One way to avoid liability is to make certain the patient's attending physician has written a proper order for the application of restraints which are actually placed on the patient. Nurses may avoid liability for false imprisonment by following proper procedures, just as officials in *Maniaci* avoided this type of liability by acting in accordance with the laws governing commitment.

Maniaci v. Marquette University,
50 Wis.2d 287, 184 N.W.2d 168 (1971)
Supreme Court of Wisconsin

In September of 1966, Saralee Maniaci left her home in
Windsor, Ontario, Canada, to attend school at Marquette
University in Milwaukee. She was sixteen years old at the
time. She arrived at the airport in Milwaukee carrying a check
for $2,000, which was to be used to pay the year's expenses.
She was met at the airport by Father Thomas A. Stemper, a
Jesuit priest employed by the university and an old Maniaci
family friend. He took her to Heraty Hall, which was to be her
dormitory.

In the following months Saralee Maniaci became very
dissatisfied with life at Marquette. She found the quality of
education unimpressive, and she was bored with her courses.
She was also unhappy with her social life. She complained to
her father about the "fast" social life at the university. She
spent three of the first seven weekends at her parents' home in
Windsor. She travelled from Milwaukee to Windsor with
Leonard McGravey, a thirty-two-year-old former priest, whom
she had known since she was in high school. Each time she went
home, she told her parents of her desire to leave Marquette.
Her father each time convinced her that things would get
better and that she should give the school another chance. She
returned to Marquette on October 30, 1966, with the idea that
she would give Marquette one more chance, but that if things
did not work out, she would have her parents' permission to quit.

On Wednesday, November 2, 1966, she decided to quit
school. She told her closest friend, Jean Huby, that she was
leaving, and Jean said she wanted to leave too. Jean asked to
go home with Saralee to Windsor, because Jean thought her
father would send her back to Marquette if she tried to go to
her own home. Saralee agreed to this request. Jean got
Saralee to promise, however, that she would not tell anyone
where they were going.

On Thursday, November 3, 1966, Saralee went to the
Student Credit Bank and withdrew the $1300 she had remaining
on deposit there. She then went to the railroad station and
purchased two tickets to Detroit, which was across the river
from Windsor by train. She then went to Heraty Hall and began
packing.

A representative of the student bank notified the dean of
women's office that Saralee had said that she was leaving
school. Assistant Dean of Women Patricia Watson notified

Esther Morgan, the head resident at Heraty Hall. Esther Morgan notified Joseph Maniaci that his daughter Saralee was intending to run away from school to marry an older man. When Maniaci learned that the man was Leonard McGravey, he said there must be some mistake and gave his approval of whatever plans Leonard McGravey had.

Esther Morgan told Saralee that on Friday morning, November 4, 1966, she was to report to the office of the dean of women. When Saralee failed to report, Dean of Women Mary Alice Cannon went with Assistant Dean Watson to Heraty Hall to persuade Saralee to remain at the school. Saralee admitted that she intended to leave Milwaukee that evening and refused to state her destination. She stated a number of reasons for leaving, including hostility toward her parents, dissatisfaction with education at the university, a desire to act, sing, and write, and a belief that she was more mature than the other students she knew. She insisted that she was going to leave by train at 8 o'clock that evening and that she would notify her father later. She did not state that she had, in fact received her father's permission to leave. The discussion continued throughout the morning.

Father Stemper was called about 11:30 a.m. to help persuade Saralee to remain at the school until her parents could be notified. Dean Cannon concluded that Student Health Physician Dean D. Miller should be called. Doctor Miller arrived at Heraty Hall at about 1:30 p.m. accompanied by Nurse June B. Steiner. Doctor Miller conferred with Saralee for about two hours. During that time, Dean Cannon and Assistant Dean Watson persuaded Jean not to leave with Saralee. Throughout the afternoon, unsuccessful attempts were made by Saralee and the dean of women to contact Saralee's father. At 3:30 p.m., Doctor Miller suggested to Dean Cannon that Saralee be hospitalized. Father Stemper saw nothing abnormal about Saralee's conduct and disagreed with Doctor Miller, although he did not know Doctor Miller proposed commitment to a mental hospital.

Milwaukee police officers were called and asked to bring the proper papers for temporary detention of Saralee Maniaci under the emergency provisions . . . The officers arrived at about 4:30 p.m. The "Application for Temporary Custody" was filled out by Doctor Miller and signed by him, by Dean Cannon, and by Nurse Steiner. The "Application for Temporary Custody" stated:

That each of the applicants is an adult resident of the State of Wisconsin, and that one of the applicants, Dean D. Miller,

M.D., is a physician licensed to practice medicine and surgery in this state.

That Saralee Maniaci of the City of Milwaukee, in said county, hereinafter called the patient, is believed to be mentally ill for the reason (state facts observed or information known tending to show existence of mental illness, mental infirmity, or mental deficiency): Saralee is a 16 yr. old freshman at Marquette University, wishes to leave the University without the consent of the University officials or her parents, to an unknown destination. Her plans for the future are indefinite and it is obvious that she cannot give rational reasons for leaving.

That the patient is in need of hospitalization and is irresponsible and dangerous to self or others, so as to require immediate temporary detention by reason of she has persuaded other girls to leave the University with her for reasons which are illogical to us. As a minor we cannot permit her to leave, and feel that she should be confined until her parents have been informed of the situation, and appear on her behalf, and until she has been thoroughly evaluated by a psychiatrist.

WHEREFORE, your applicants pray for immediate temporary detention of the patient in the custody of the sheriff or other police officer, not exceeding five days, and for a judicial inquiry to determine the mental condition of the patient and for such orders of temporary or permanent nature as may be necessary.

Dean D. Miller M.D.	1945 Wauwatosa Avenue Wauwatosa, Wisc.
Mary Alice Cannon	731 Glenview Avenue Wauwatosa
June B. Steiner, RN	3731 W. Linden Place Milwaukee

The police officers took Saralee to the Milwaukee County General Hospital, where she was taken to a locked ward on the fifth floor for mental observation. The officers said they had an intelligent conversation with Saralee and that she was cooperative and displayed no tendencies toward violence.

At the hospital her clothes were removed and she was given a bath. She was checked for scars or bruises and given a housecoat to wear. She stated that while confined to a room with several other female persons, she saw what appeared to be shocking conduct by two female persons in the same bed.

She persuaded a social worker at the hospital to notify Leonard McGravey what had happened to her. At about 11 p.m., McGravey arrived at the hospital and was permitted to talk to Saralee after she told the nurse he was her fiance. She told him what had happened, and he relayed the message to her father. Her father contacted Doctor Miller and insisted that his daughter be released. Doctor Miller was unable to have Saralee released at that time of night, but he arranged to have Saralee transferred from a large ward on the fifth floor to a locked private room. Doctor Miller did not tell Joseph Maniaci that Saralee would continue to be confined in a mental hospital. She was, however, released from the hospital at about 9 o'clock the next morning. She returned to her dormitory, gathered her belongings, and went to Windsor. She never returned to Marquette . . .

Plaintiffs, respondents herein, take the position that the facts spelled out a cause of action for false imprisonment, that the verdict is supported by sufficient evidence, and that the damages found by the jury were reasonable.

We agree with the defendants in their contention that no cause of action has been proved under the theory of false imprisonment.

This court has defined the tort of false imprisonment as, " 'The unlawful restraint by one person of the physical liberty of another.' " It is apparent, therefore, that a "lawful" restrain does not constitute false imprisonment, though it may well constitute some other tort.

In the instant case it is clear that the type of tort that the concept of "false imprisonment" encompasses did not take place. There was not an "unlawful" restraint of freedom.

Since the plaintiff Saralee was confined pursuant to the mandate of [the statute] and by a petition that conformed, prima facie at least, to the jurisdictional requirements of the statute, the confinement was pursuant to law. She was arrested by legal process in the sense that the document executed by the defendants under the statute conferred authority or jurisdiction upon the police officers to take physical custody of the plaintiff's person and to deliver her to the mental hospital . . .

Judgment is reversed . . .and cause is remanded for such other and further action and proceedings as may be consistent with this opinion and for a new trial.

o **Recap of the Case.** As a practical matter, any limitation of a patient's freedom of movement, including the application of restraints to the patient, should be examined carefully from the point of view of liability for false imprisonment. As this case illustrates, the key concern for nurses is to make certain that their limitation of patients' freedom of movement is lawful at all times.

9

Infliction of Emotional Distress/Extreme and Outrageous Conduct

Practitioners are liable under this theory when three conditions are met: 1) their conduct goes beyond that usually tolerated by society; 2) their conduct is calculated to cause mental distress; and 3) their conduct actually causes severe mental distress. In some states, members of patients' immediate families who witness the conduct may also recover.

PRACTITIONER NOT LIABLE FOR INFLICTION OF EMOTIONAL DISTRESS

The basic principles of this type of liability are presented in *Grimsley v. Samson*, 85 Wash.2d, 52, 530 P.2d 291 (1975).

Grimsley v. Samson, 85 Wash.2d, 52, 530 P.2d 291 (1975)
Supreme Court of Washington

. . . Plaintiff alleged he was the husband of the decedent and that a patient–physician relationship existed between Dr. Samson and the deceased. He asserted further that the doctor negligently, recklessly, wantonly and outrageously breached that relationship by abandoning her and failing to provide her with medical care. Plaintiff pleaded further that as a direct and proximate result thereof he "was required to witness the terrifying agony and explicit pain and suffering of his wife while she proceeded to die right in front of his eyes . . . thereby proximately causing severe damage to [plaintiff including] . . . mental anguish and pain and suffering . . .and which has further resulted in physical injury and deterioration in . . . plaintiff, and that . . . plaintiff has been damaged . . . both emotionally and physically . . ."

Concerning the defendant hospital, plaintiff alleged he was the husband of the deceased and that a patient–hospital relationship existed between it and his wife. Similarly, the hospital is alleged to have negligently, recklessly, and wantonly breached its duty to provide required medical care and services to the deceased despite plaintiff's requests therefor. Plaintiff alleges "that as direct and proximate result of said outrageous conduct [he] had inflicted upon him the most severe and damaging emotional and physical distress and anguish . . ."

Plaintiff has two basic theories, either of which he contends support his claim for relief. The first is based upon the rationale of *Dillon v. Legg.* In *Dillon* a mother, whose child was struck by defendant's vehicle, was not within the traditional "zone of danger" at the time of the incident. She did, however, see the car strike the child as it was allegedly being driven by defendant in a negligent manner. The mother suffered a severe emotional disturbance. The California Supreme Court recognized that injury, standing alone, imposes no liability. Nevertheless, it found that a duty existed and recognized the right of the mother (a third party) to recover, apparently based upon a theory that liability to such third person, (i.e., the mother) would exist if a defendant should have foreseen that a mother would be in the vicinity of her child and would be disturbed by an injury to her child. In discussing the subject of "foreseeability" and consequent "duty" the California Court stressed (1) the mother's close proximity to the scene of the accident; (2) the shock having resulted from a direct emotional impact upon her from the sensory and contemporaneous observance of the accident, as contrasted with learning of it from others after its occurence; and (3) the close mother–child relationship. The court also limited its holding to the case in which a "plaintiff suffered a shock which resulted in physical injury . . ." . . .

. . .[T]he California courts quickly extended the rationale of *Dillon* to a parent who had not witnessed the accident. The year following *Dillon*, a mother was allowed recovery although she did not actually witness her child's accident. She came upon the scene moments after the accident occurred. Thus, within a short period of time, the element of foreseeability was broadened and extended and with it the nature of the duty owed to third parties . . . [E]ven assuming there are cogent reasons for extending liability in favor of victims of shock resulting from injury to others, there appears to be no rational way to restrict the scope of liability even as attempted by *Dillon's* three limiting standards. None are of much help if they are expected to serve the purpose of holding a strict rein on liability if the test is to be "reasonably objective."

. . .We, too, follow the majority view and reject the *Dillon* concept.

Having rejected *Dillon* we return to appellant's second theory. He argues that while a defendant might not be accountable for mere negligent actions which cause emotional stress, one, who by extreme and outrageous conduct, intentionally or recklessly directed at a third person, causes severe emotional distress to a member of such person's immediate family, should be liable if the person so affected is present at the time . . .

As a general rule, we have denied recovery for mental anguish and distress in cases not involving malice or wrongful intent, unless there has been an actual invasion of a plaintiff's person or security, or a direct possibility thereof . . . Two major considerations generally referred to are: (1) the likelihood that courts will be flooded by fraudulent claims and (2) the defendant's potentially unlimited liability for every type of mental disturbance.

. . . The argument of possible fraud in suits for mental distress "presupposes that courts are so ineffectual and the jury system is so imperfect that fraudulent claims cannot be distinguished from the legitimate." We do not subscribe to this pessimistic premise . . .

The second argument, that a defendant will have potentially unlimited liability for every type of mental disturbance, is we feel, adequately met . . . First, the emotional distress must be inflicted intentionally or recklessly; mere negligence is not enough. Second, the conduct of the defendant must be outrageous and extreme . . . [I]t is not enough that a "defendant has acted with an intent which is tortious or even criminal, or that he has intended to inflict emotional distress, or even that his conduct has been characterized by 'malice,' or a degree of aggravation which would entitle the plaintiff to punitive damages for another tort." Liability exists "only where the conduct has been so outrageous in character, and so extreme in degree, as to go beyond all possible bounds of decency, and to be regarded as atrocious, and utterly intolerable in a civilized community." [L]iability in the tort of outrage "does not extend to mere insults, indignities, threats, annoyances, petty oppressions, or other trivialities." In this area plaintiffs must necessarily be hardened to a certain degree of rough language, unkindness and lack of consideration. Clearly a case by case approach will be necessary to define the precise limits of such conduct. Nevertheless, among the factors a jury or court should consider are the positions occupied by the defendant . . . whether plaintiff was peculiarly susceptible to emotional distress and defendant's knowledge of this fact . . . and whether defendant's conduct may have been privileged under the circumstances . . .

Third, the conduct must result in severe emotional distress to the plaintiff . . . Resulting bodily harm would, of course, be an indication of severe emotional distress, but a showing of bodily harm is not necessary. Fourth, the plaintiff must be an immediate family member of the person who is the object of the defendant's actions, and he must be present at the time of such conduct . . .

Turning to plaintiff's complaint, we find that it states a cause of action . . .It is alleged that defendant's conduct was reckless and wanton; that it was outrageous in that plaintiff "was required to witness the terrifying agony and explicit pain and suffering of his wife while she proceeded to die right in front of his eyes and at all times remaining helpless because of his inability to secure any medical care or treatment for his wife at all . . ." Finally, this conduct on the part of the defendants is alleged to have caused plaintiff severe mental anguish which has resulted in physical injury . . .

The order of dismissal is reversed and the case remanded to the trial court for further proceedings.

PRACTITIONERS LIABLE FOR INFLICTION OF EMOTIONAL DISTRESS DUE TO FAILURE TO DELIVER LIVE INFANT DESPITE FATHER'S PROTEST

Austin v. The Regents of the University of California, 89 Calif.App.3d 354, 152, Cal.Rptr. 420 (1979) provides an example of the extreme circumstances necessary to successfully make a claim for damages based upon infliction of emotional distress. In this case, plaintiff was present in the delivery room for the birth of his child. During delivery, his wife died. Plaintiff then asked the attending physicians and nurses to deliver the child because he could tell that the child was alive. They refused, and plaintiff experienced the death of his child by feeling his wife's body. The court decided in plaintiff's favor.

Austin v. The Regents of the University of California,
89 Calif.App.3d 354, 152 Cal.Rptr.420 (1979)
California Court of Appeals

. . . Plaintiff's wife was a patient of defendants for the purpose of delivery of their child. The wife died during the delivery procedure. After her death, plaintiff, who was in the delivery room, was able to feel life in the as yet unborn child; he asked the attending physician and nurses to deliver the child but they refused; the child died, and plaintiff was able to ascertain the death by feeling the wife's body.

The first cause of action seeks to recover for the emotional distress resulting from the death of the child. The rulings here complained of were to the effect that, on the facts above stated, there was no cause of action for emotional distress. We disagree.

The elements of a cause of action for emotional distress were thus stated in the seminal case of *Dillon v. Legg* . . .

We note, first, that we deal with a case in which plaintiff suffered a shock which resulted in physical injury and we confine our ruling to that case. In determining, in such a case, whether defendant should reasonably foresee the injury to plaintiff, or, in other terminology, whether defendant owes plaintiff a duty of due care, the courts will take into account such factors as the following: 1) Whether plaintiff was located near the scene of the accident as contrasted with one who was a distance away from it. 2) Whether the shock resulted from a direct emotional impact upon plaintiff from the sensory and contemporaneous observance of the accident, as contrasted with learning of the accident from others after its occurence. 3) Whether plaintiff and the victim were closely related, as contrasted with an absence of any relationship or the presence of only a distant relationship.

The trial court, and respondents here, relied on the decision of the Supreme Court in *Justus v. Atchison* . . . In *Justus*, all the plaintiff claimed was that he was in the delivery room when the defendant improperly conducted a delivery. The Supreme Court denied relief solely on the ground that, on the facts alleged, plaintiff did not, and could not, have seen any allegedly negligent acts of delivery and that his distress arose only after the death when he was told of it by the defendant doctor. Here, however, plaintiff alleges that he learned of the death by his own observation of the cessation of life in the fetus and that his shock and distress were occasioned by that sensory and contemporaneous realization of the death. *Justus* is not here applicable. Since the presence of the other two elements required by *Dillon*—presence at the scene and relationship—are not disputed, it follows that the first cause of action did state, and the declarations filed on the motion for summary judgment show, a triable cause of action . . .

o **Recap of the Cases.** The key to avoiding liability for infliction of emotional distress is avoidance of any behavior by nurses which could be characterized as extreme and outrageous. While a determination of what constitutes extreme and outrageous conduct is somewhat subjective, most people agree that allowing an infant to die in utero as the child's father begs for a caesarean delivery is extreme and outrageous. Nurses should use this case as a benchmark against which to judge whether certain other behaviors may be extreme and outrageous.

10

Invasion of Privacy

When practitioners subject their patients to unwanted publicity, they may be liable for invasion of privacy.

OBSERVATION OF PATIENTS BY UNAUTHORIZED PERSONS CONSTITUTES INVASION OF PRIVACY

In a Michigan case, *De May v. Roberts*, 46 Mich. 160, 9 N.W. 146 (1881), a practitioner was found liable for an invasion of the patient's privacy when the practitioner allowed a "lay" friend to observe the delivery of the patient's child. While this case is an old one, the basic principles are applicable today. If nurses allow unauthorized persons to observe patients, they may still be liable for invasion of the patient's privacy.

De May v. Roberts, 46 Mich. 160, 9 N.W. 146 (1881)
Supreme Court of Michigan

The declaration in this case in the first count sets forth that the plaintiff was at a time and place named a poor married woman, and being confined in child–bed and a stranger, employed in a professional capacity defendant De May who was a physician; that defendant visited the plaintiff as such, and against her desire and intending to deceive her wrongfully, etc., introduced and caused to be present at the house and lying–in room of the plaintiff and while she was in the pains of parturition the defendant Scattergood, who intruded upon the

161

privacy of the plaintiff, indecently, wrongfully and unlawfully laid hands upon and assaulted her, the said Scattergood, which was well known to defendant De May, being a young unmarried man, a stranger to the plaintiff and utterly ignorant of the practice of medicine, while the plaintiff believed that he was an assistant physician, a competent and proper person to be present and to aid her in her extremity . . .

The evidence on the part of the plaintiff tended to prove the allegations of the declaration. On the part of the defendants evidence was given tending to prove that Scattergood very reluctantly accompanied Dr. De May at the urgent request of the latter; that the night was a dark and stormy one, the roads over which they had to travel in getting to the house of the plaintiff were so bad that a horse could not be rode or driven over them; that the doctor was sick and very much fatigued from overwork, and therefore asked the defendant Scattergood to accompany and assist him in carrying a lantern, umbrella and certain articles deemed necessary upon such occasions; that upon arriving at the house of the plaintiff the doctor knocked, and when the door was opended by the husband of the plaintiff, De May said to him, "that I had fetched a friend along to help carry my things;" he, plaintiff's husband, said all right, and seemed to be perfectly satisfied. They were bid to enter, treated kindly and no objection whatever made to the presence of defendant Scattergood. That while there Scattergood, at Dr. De May's request, took hold of plaintiff's hand and held her during a paroxysm of pain, and that both of the defendants in all respects throughout acted in a proper and becoming manner actuated by a sense of duty and kindness.

Some preliminary questions were raised during the progress of the trial which may first be considered. The plaintiff when examined as a witness was asked, what idea she entertained in reference to Scattergood's character and right to be in the house during the time he was there, and answered that she thought he was a student or a physician. To this there could be no legal objection. It was not only important to know the character in which Scattergood went there, but to learn what knowledge the plaintiff had upon that subject. It was not claimed that the plaintiff or her husband, who were strangers in that vicinity, had ever met Scattergood before this time or had any knowledge or information concerning him beyond what they obtained on that evening, and it was claimed by the defendant that both the plaintiff and her husband must have known, from certain ambiguous expressions used, that he was not a physician.

We are of the opinion that the plaintiff and her husband had a right to presume that a practicing physician would not, upon an occasion of that character, take with him and introduce into the house, a young man in no way, either by education or otherwise, connected with the medical profession; and that something more clear and certain as to his non–professional character would be required to put the plaintiff and her husband upon their guard, or remove such presumption, than the remark made by De May that he had brought a friend along to help carry his things. The plaintiff was not bound however to rest her case upon this presumption, however strong it might be considered, but had a right to prove what she supposed was the fact, and this she could do by showing anything said at the time having such a tendency, or in the absence thereof what she actually believed to be the fact . . .

A few facts which were undisputed may assist in more clearly presenting the remaining question. Upon the morning of January 3d Dr. De May was called to visit the plaintiff professionally which he did at her house. This house was 14 by 16 feet. A partition ran partly across one end thus forming a place for a bed or bedroom, but there was no door to this bedroom. Next to this so–called bedroom, and between the partition and side of the house, there was what is known and designated as a bed sink, here there was a bed with a curtain in front of it, and it was in this bed the doctor found Mrs. Roberts when he made his first visit. On their way to the house that night De May told Scattergood, who knew that the plaintiff was about to be confined, "how the house was; that she was in the bed sink lock, and there was a curtain in front of her, and told him he need not see her at all." When the defendants got to the house they found Mrs. Roberts "had moved from the bed sink and was lying on the lounge near the stove."

I now quote further from the testimony of Dr. De May as to what took place: "I made an examination of Mrs. Roberts and found no symptoms of labor at all, any more than there was the previous morning. I told them that I had been up several nights and was tired and would like to lie down awhile; previous to this, however, some one spoke about supper, and supper was got and Scattergood and myself ate supper, and then went to bed. I took off my pants and had them hung up by the stove to dry; Scattergood also laid down with his clothes on. We lay there an hour or more, and Scattergood shook me and informed me that they had called me and wanted me. Scattergood got my pants and then went and sat down by the stove and placed his feet on a pile of wood that lay beside the stove, with his face towards the wall of the house and his back partially toward the couch on which Mrs. Roberts was lying. I made an examination and found that the lady has having labor pains. Her husband stood at her head to assist her; Mrs. Parks upon one side, and I went to the foot of the couch. During her pains Mrs. Roberts had kicked Mrs. Parks in the pit of the stomach, and Mrs. Parks got up and went out doors, and while away and about the time she was coming in, Mrs. Roberts was subjected to another labor pain and commenced rocking herself and throwing her arms, and I said catch her, to Scattergood, and he jumped right up and came over to her and caught her by the hand and stayed there a short time, and then Mrs. Parks came up and took her place again, and Scattergood got up and went and took his place again, back by the stove. In a short time the child was born. Scattergood took no notice of her while sitting by the stove. The child was properly cared for; Mrs. Roberts was properly cared for, dressed and carried and placed in bed. I left some medicine to be given her in case she should suffer from pains."

Dr. De May therefore took an unprofessional young unmarried man with him, introduced and permitted him to remain in the house of the plaintiff, when it was apparent that he could hear at least, if not see all that was said and done . . .without either the plaintiff or her husband having any knowledge or reason to believe the true character of such third party. It would be shocking to our sense of right, justice and propriety to doubt even but that for such an act the law would afford an ample remedy. To the plaintiff the occasion was a most sacred one and no one had a right to intrude unless invited or because of some real and pressing necessity which it is not pretended existed in this case. The plaintiff had a legal right to the privacy of her apartment at such a time, and the law secures to her this right by requiring others to observe it, and to abstain from its violation. The fact that at the time, she consented to the presence of Scattergood supposing him to be a physician, does not preclude her from maintaining an action and recovering substantial damages upon afterwards ascertaining his true character. In obtaining admission at such a time and under such circumstances without fully disclosing his true character, both parties were guilty of deceit, and the wrong thus done entitles the injured party to recover the damages afterwards sustained, from shame and moritfication upon discovering the true character of the defendants. . .

o **Recap of the Case.** Nurses should not be misled by the old–fashioned language of this case. They must be aware of the need to protect the patient's privacy at all times. A good rule to apply to every situation is that only staff with a legitimate need to observe or become involved in the patient's care should be allowed to do so.

A Note About Defenses
to Intentional Torts

There are two primary defenses to a claim that a practitioner has committed an intentional tort: 1) lack of intent; and 2) consent. Only practitioners who engage in intentional conduct are liable, by definition, under the theories summarized above. Conduct is intentional if, at a minimum, it is voluntary conduct. Thus, if a nurse became unconscious while treating a patient, resulting in injury to the patient, the nurse is not liable under intentional tort theories because her conduct was not voluntary. By the same token, if the patient has consented to the conduct which results in injury with a full understanding of the risks of injury likely to be incurred, the practitioner will not be liable.

Consent by the patient to routine and non–routine medical care is required prior to rendering treatment. The most important principal governing consent is that individuals have the right to control their bodies. The clearest expression of this principle appears in *Schloendorff v. Society of New York Hospitals*, 211 N.Y. 125, 105 N.E. 92 (1914) *overruled on other grounds*, and *Bing v. Thunig*, 2 N.Y. 2d656, 143 N.E. 2d 3, 163 N.Y.S.2d 3 (1957), a case concerning consent to surgery. In the decision in *Schloendorff,* Justice Cardozo stated:

> Every human being of adult years and sound mind has a right to determine what shall be done with his own body and a surgeon who performs an operation without his patient's consent commits an assault for which he is liable in damages . . .

More specifically, consent requires the presence of three elements: 1) capacity; 2) information; 3) voluntariness. All three requirements must be met in order to obtain the consent of the patient. Historically, health professionals have focused almost all of their attention on the evidence that information about treatment was conveyed to the patient: the consent form. Every nurse has seen these forms which are signed by the patient and then become part of the patient's medical record. The traditional attitude is that everything with regard to consent to treatment is "OK" as long as the patient signs the form and it appears in the chart.

In fact, this attitude results in a completely false sense of security. Practitioners must redirect their attention from the consent form which functions as evidence that information concerning treatment was conveyed to the actual process of conveying information. In other words, the consent form will protect providers from liability only if it is a reflection of a dialogue between treating professional and patient. If no discussion or an incomplete exchange occurred, the execution of the consent form is absolutely meaningless because a crucial element of consent is missing. Information regarding treatment was not actually given to the patient.

For a comprehensive discussion of the principles governing consent, and practical suggestions for obtaining valid informed consents, see the companion volume to this book, Hogue, Elizabeth E., *Nursing and Informed Consent*, National Health Publishing, 1985.

Conclusion

As these materials illustrate, the issue of liability for treatment is a complex one. Knowledge of the process and an understanding of the issues encourages practitioners to take the matter of professional responsibility seriously and to learn to limit their risks as far as possible. Nevertheless, as Judge Kelleher pointed out in *Wilkinson v. Vesey*, 295 A.2d 676, 690 (R.I., October 20, 1972), building good relations with patients is "good medicine," "good humanity," "good public relations," and "good medicolegal defense." In the midst of legal issues and technical discussions, nurses must not lose sight of this most important aspect of risk management. If practitioner–patient rapport is high, patients are much less likely to sue their practitioner.

How to Read a Citation

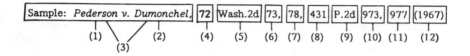

Key:

(1)   The name of the plaintiff at the trial court level. The name of
      the appellant in a case before a court of appeals.

(2)   The name of the defendant at the trial court level. The name of
      the appellee in a case before a court of appeals.

(3)   The names of the plaintiff and defendant or the appellant and
      appellee constitute the name of the case.

(4)   Indicates the number of the book in which the case appears.

(5)   Indicates the name of the series of books in which the case
      appears.

(6)   Designates the page number on which the case begins.

(7)   States the number of the page on which the specific portion of the
      case referred to by the court begins.

(8)   Many cases are published in more than one series of books. This
      indicates the number of a second book in which this case appears.

(9)   Indicates the name of another series of books in which this case
      also appears.

(10) Designates the page number on which the case begins in the
      second book in which the case appears.

(11) States the page number in the second book on which the case
      begins.

(12) States the year in which the case was decided.

171

Glossary

The author relied heavily upon *Black's Law Dictionary*, 5th Edition, West Publishing Co., 1979, To prepare this glossary. Readers should make further use of this excellent resource when necessary.

Actual damages. Compensation for actual injuries or losses such as medical expenses, lost wages, etc.

Affidavit. A written statement of facts given voluntarily under oath.

Allegation. The written statements by a party to a suit concerning what the party expects to prove.

Amended complaint. A corrected or revised version of the document filed in court by the plaintiff to begin a suit.

Amicus curiae. Literally, "friend of the court." Person or organizations with a strong interest in or views on a suit may ask the court in which the suit is filed for permission to file a brief to suggest a resolution of the case consistent with their views. *Amicus curiae* briefs are often filed in appeals of cases involving a broad public interest such as civil rights cases.

Appellant. The party who appeals the decision of one court to another court.

Appellate brief. Written arguments by attorneys required to be filed with an appellate court stating the reasons why the trial court acted correctly (appellee's brief) or incorrectly (appellant's brief). The contents and form of appellate briefs are often prescribed by the rules of various court systems.

Appellate briefs usually contain a statement of issues presented for review by the appellate court, a statement of the case, argument, and a conclusion stating the precise action sought by the party submitting the brief.

Appellate review. Examination of a previous proceeding.

Appellee. The party in a case against whom an appeal is brought. Sometimes also called the "respondent."

Assault. Any conduct which creates a reasonable apprehension of being touched in an injurious manner. No actual touching is required to prove assault.

Assumption of the risk. A defense to plaintiffs' claims based on the theory that plaintiffs may not recover for injuries to which they consent. In order to prove that the plaintiff assumed the risk, the defendant must show that: (1) the plaintiff had knowledge of a dangerous condition, (2) the plaintiff appreciated the nature or extent of the danger, and (3) the plaintiff voluntarily exposed himself to the danger.

Attorney in fact. Any person authorized by another to act in his place either for a particular purpose or for the transaction of business affairs in general. This authority is conferred by a document called a power of attorney.

Battery. An unconsented, actual touching which causes injury.

Borrowed servant rule. A theory of liability or negligence which is used to extend liability beyond the person who actually committed negligent acts to include those who had the right of control over the negligent actions.

Brief. A written statement prepared by an attorney arguing a case in court. A brief contains a summary of the facts of the case, the pertinent laws, and an argument of how the law applies to the facts supporting an attorney's position.

Burden of proof. The requirement of proving facts in dispute on an issue raised between the parties in a case.

Captain of the ship doctrine. This doctrine imposes liability on surgeons in charge of operations for negligence of assistants during periods when those assistants are under the surgeons' control, even though the assistants are also employees of a hospital. This doctrine extends the borrowed servant rule to the operating rooms of hospitals.

Cause of action. The fact or facts which give a person the right to begin a suit.

Common law. As opposed to laws created by legislatures, the common law consists of legal principles based solely on usages and customs of time immemorial, particularly the ancient unwritten law of England.

Complaint. The first document filed in court by the plaintiff to begin a suit.

Conservator. Any individual appointed by a court to manage the affairs of an incompetent person.

Continuance. Adjournment or postponement of a session, hearing, trial, or other proceeding to a subsequent day or time.

Contributory negligence. A defense to a claim of negligence. Any act or omission on the part of the complaining party amounting to a breach of the duty the law imposes on everyone to protect themselves from injury which contributes to the injury complained of by the plaintiff.

Counterclaim. Claim presented by a defendant in opposition to the claim of the plaintiff. If the defendant establishes his claim, it will defeat or diminish the plaintiff's claim.

Cross–complaint. A defendant or cross–defendant (plaintiff) may file a cross–complaint based on: (1) any claim against any of the parties who filed the complaint against him *or* (2) any claim against a person alleged to be liable whether or not the person is already a party to the suit. The claims in a cross–complaint must: (1) arise out of the same transaction or occurrence as the original suit *and* (2) must make a claim or assert a right or interest in property or controversy which is the basis for the claim already made.

Cross–defendants. Plaintiffs who, subsequent to suing defendants, are then counter–sued by the defendants. Defendants in a suit brought by defendants.

Cross–examination. The questioning of a witness by an adverse party to test the truth of his testimony or to further develop it.

Declaratory judgment. Provided for in state and federal statutes. A person may seek a declaratory judgment from a court if there is an actual controversy among the parties, and the party asking for the declaratory judgment has some question or doubt about his legal rights. The judgment is binding on the parties both presently and in the future.

Defendant. The person defending or denying; the party against whom a civil lawsuit is brought or the accused in a criminal case.

Defense. A response to the claims of the other party stating the reasons why the claims should not be recognized.

Demurrer. An argument in which the defendant admits the facts in the plaintiff's complaint, but claims that the facts are insufficient to require a response.

Deposition. Advice by which one party asks oral questions of the other party or of a witness for the other party before the trial begins. The person who answers questions is called a deponent. The deposition is conducted under oath outside of the courtroom, usually in one of the lawyer's offices. A transcript or word–for–word account is made of the deposition.

Directed verdict. When the party with the burden of proof fails to prove all necessary elements of the case, the trial judge may direct a verdict in favor of the other party, since there can only be one result anyway.

Docket. A list or calendar of cases to be tried during a particular period of time prepared by employees of the court for use by the court and attorneys.

Due process clause. Two clauses in the United States Constitution, one in the Fifth Amendment applicable to the United States Government, the other in the Fourteenth Amendment which protects persons from actions by the states. There are two aspects: (1) procedural, in which a person is guaranteed fair procedures, and (2) substantive, which protects a person's property from unfair governmental interference. Similary clauses are in most state constitutions.

Due process of law. An orderly proceeding in which a person receives notice of the proceeding and the subject matter of the proceeding, and is given an opportunity to be heard and to enforce and protect his rights before a court or person(s) with power to hear and determine the case.

En banc. Full bench. Refers to a session in which all the judges of a court participate in deciding a case, rather than one judge or a regular panel of judges.

Equal protection clause. A provision in the Fourteenth Amendment to the United States Constitution which requires every state to treat individuals in similar circumstances the same in terms of rights and redress of improper actions against them.

Ex parte. On one side only; by or for one party; done for, on behalf of, or on the application of, one party only. A judicial proceeding, order, injunction, etc. is *ex parte* when it is granted at the request of and for the benefit of one party only without notice to any person adversely interested.

False imprisonment. A tort which consists of intentionally confining a person without his consent.

Felony. A crime of a more serious nature. Under federal law and many state statutes, a felony is any offense punishable by death or imprisonment for a term exceeding one year.

Guardian.. Any person responsible for taking care of managing the property of and protecting the rights of another person who, because of youth or lack of understanding, is incapable of managing his own affairs.

Guardian ad litem. A special guardian appointed by a court to prosecute or defend, on behalf of a minor or incompetent, a suit to which he is a party.

Harmless error. Any trivial error or an error which is merely academic because it did not affect important rights of any party to a case and did not affect the final result of the case. Harmless error will not serve as a basis for changing a decision of the court.

Implied consent. Signs, actions or facts, or inaction or silence, which indicate that consent is given.

In loco parentis. In the place of a parent; instead of a parent; charged with a parent's rights, duties, and responsibilities.

Infliction of emotional distress. Conduct going beyond that usually tolerated by society which is calculated to cause mental distress *and* which actually causes severe mental distress.

Informed consent. A person's agreement to allow something to happen that is based on a full disclosure of facts needed to make the decision intelligently.

Intent. Design, resolve, or determination which serves as the basis for a person's actions. Intent can rarely be proven directly but may be inferred from the circumstances.

Interrogatories. A tool to elicit information important to a case prior to trial. Interrogatories are written questions about the case submitted by one party to another party or witness. The answers to interrogatories are usually given under oath, i.e., the person answering the questions signs a sworn statement that the answers are true.

Judge a quo. Literally, "from which." A judge of a court from which a case was taken before a decision is made.

Judgment of nonsuit. A decision by a court against plaintiffs when they are unable to prove their cases or refuse or neglect to proceed to trial. A court decision which leaves the issues undetermined.

Judgment notwithstanding the verdict (j.n.o.v.). A judgment entered by order of the court for a party, even though the jury decided in favor of the other party. A motion for directed verdict must usually be made prior to a judgment, notwithstanding the verdict.

Jurisdiction. The right and power of a court to decide a particular case.

Jury instructions. Statements made by the judge to the jury regarding the law applicable to the case the jury is considering which the jury is required to accept and apply. Attorneys for both sides usually furnish the judge with suggested instructions.

Justiciable controversy. Courts will only decide justiciable controversies. That is, courts will only decide cases in which there is a real, substantial difference of opinion between the parties as opposed to a hypothetical difference or dispute or one that is academic or moot.

Leave to amend. Permission or authorization given by a judge to any party to a suit to correct or reverse any document filed by the party with the court.

Locality rule. In order to show negligence, according to the locality rule, a plaintiff must prove that the defendant practitioner failed to render care considered reasonable in the same or in a similar geographical location.

Misdemeanor. Criminal offenses less serious than a felony and usually punished by fine or imprisonment other than in a penitentiary. Any criminal offense other than a felony.

Motion for new trial. Request to a judge to set aside a decision already made in a case and to order a new trial on the basis that the first decision was improper or unfair.

Motion for summary judgment. An application made to a court or judge to obtain a ruling or order that all or part of the other party's claim or defense should be eliminated from further consideration. This motion is made when a party believes there is no significant disagreement concerning important facts among the parties *and* the law supports the position of the party making the motion. A motion for summary judgment may be directed toward all or part of a claim or defense. It may be made on the basis of the pleadings or other portions of the record in the case, or it may be supported by affidavits and a variety of outside material.

Motion to dismiss. An application made to a court or judge to obtain or order that the plaintiff's suit should be eliminated from further consideration by the court or judge. This motion is usually made before a trial is held and may be based on a variety of reasons, such as the insufficiency of the plaintiff's claims, improper service of process of the plaintiff's suit on the defendant, etc.

Motion to intervene/Plea in intervention. A written request to a court to become a party to a case filed in the court based upon an interest in the results of the case.

Negligence. The failure to do something a reasonable person would do or doing something a reasonable person would not do.

Nominal damages. A very small amount of money awarded to plaintiffs in cases in which there is no substantial injury. Nominal damages are awarded to recognize technial invasions of rights or breaches of duty or in cases where the injury is more substantial but the plaintiff fails to prove the amount.

Parens patriae. Literally, "parent of the country." Refers to the role of each state as sovereign and guardian of persons under legal disability. This concept is the basis for activity by states to protect interests such as the health, comfort, and welfare of the people.

Per quod. Literally, "whereby." A phrase used to designate facts concerning the consequences of defendant's actions on the plaintiff which serve as the basis for an award of special damages to the plaintiff.

Petition. A formal, written request to a court asking the court to take certain action regarding a particular matter.

Physician–patient privilege. The right of patients not to reveal or have revealed by their physicians the communications made between patients and physicians. The privilege is established in most states and, therefore, varies from state to state. The privilege belongs only to the patient and may be waived by the patient.

Plaintiff. A person who sues in a civil case.

Pleading. The formal, written statements by the parties to a suit of their respective claims and defenses.

Power of attorney. A document authorizing another person to act on one's behalf. The other person is called the attorney in fact. The power of the attorney in fact is revoked on the death of the person who signed the power of attorney. The powers given to the attorney in fact may be general or for special purposes.

Prejudicial error. Any error which substantially affects the legal rights and obligations of a party. A prejudicial error may result in a new trial and the reversal of a decision by the court.

Pre-trial conference. A meeting between opposing attorneys and the judge in a particular case. The purpose of the meeting is to define the key issues of the case, to secure stipulations, and to take all other steps necessary to aid in the disposition of the case. Such conferences are called at the discretion of the court. The decisions made at the conference are included in a written order which controls the future course of the case.

Pre-trial discovery. Any device used by parties prior to trial to obtain evidence for use at trial such as interrogatories, depostions, requests for admission of facts, etc.

Prima facie case. Sufficient evidence presented by the plaintiff upon which a decision that the plaintiff's claims are valid can be reasonably made.

Proximate cause. The dominant cause or the cause producing injury. Any action producing injury, unbroken by any efficient intervening cause, and without which the injury would not have occurred.

Punitive damages. Money awarded to the Plaintiff over and above compensation for actual losses. Punitive damages are awarded in cases where the wrongdoing was aggravated by violence, oppression, malice, fraud, or wickedness. They are intended to compensate for mental anguish, shame, degradation, or to punish or make an example of the defendant.

Remand. To send back. The sending back of a case by an appellate court to the court in which it was previously considered in order to have some further action taken on it.

Request for admissions. Written statements of fact concerning a case which are submitted by the attorney for a party to a suit to the attorney for another party to the suit.

The attorney who receives the request is required to either admit or deny each of the statements of fact submitted. Those statements which are admitted will be treated by the court as established and need not be proved at trial.

Res ipsa loquitur. Literally, the thing speaks for itself. Although the plaintiffs cannot testify to the exact cause of injury, they can prove (1) that the instrument causing injury was in defendants' exclusive control and (2) that the injury they sustained does not normally occur in the absence of negligence. Plaintiffs who prove both of these things can recover damages for negligence even though the exact circumstances of injury are known.

Res judicata. A legal principle which says that once a *final* decision is made on a matter, the same question may not be raised at a later date.

Respondent superior. Literally, let the master say. A basis for extending liability to include the employer for the wrongful acts of employees. The doctrine is inapplicable where injury occurs while the employee is acting outside the legitimate scope of employment.

Re-trial. A new trial of a case which has already been tried at least once.

Stare decisis. Literally, "to abide by or adhere to decided cases." The policy of courts in the United States to apply previously established principles of law to all future cases where the facts are substantially the same, even though the parties to the suit are not the same.

State action. Activity of a state necessary to trigger the protection of the Fourteenth Amendment of the United States Constitution for private citizens.

Statute of limitations. Legislative enactments establishing limits on the right to sue. Statutes of limitations declare that no one may sue unless the suit is filed within a specified period of time after the occurrence or injury which is the basis for the suit.

Stay. A stopping by order of a court. A suspension of the case or some designated proceedings in it. A stay is a kind of injunction with which a court freezes its proceedings at a particular point. It can be used to stop the case altogether or to hold up only some phase of it.

Stipulation. A voluntary agreement between opposing attorneys concerning disposition of a point which alleviates the need for proof of this point or for consideration of this point by the court. This agreement is usually in the form of a written document signed by the attorneys for all of the parties and placed on file as part of the court record.

Third party defendant. A party brought into a suit by the defendant who was not a party to the transaction upon which the suit is based, but whose rights and liabilities may be affected by the suit.

Tort. A private or civil wrong or injury for which a court may award damages. Any civil suit except a suit for breach of contract. Three elements of every tort claim are: (1) existence of a legal duty by the defendant to the plaintiff, (2) breach of this duty, *and* (3) resulting damage to the plaintiff.

Transcript. A word–for–word written record of a trial, hearing, or other proceeding.

Trial. An examination and determination of issues between the parties to a case by a court.

Trial by court or judge. A trial before a judge only in contrast to a trial before a judge *and* jury.

Trial court. Judicial examination and determination of issues between the parties in a case.

Vicarious liability. Indirect legal responsibility.

Voir dire. Literally, "to speak the truth." Refers to the preliminary questioning which the court or attorneys conduct to determine the qualifications of a person to serve as a juror in a particular case.

Writ of certiorari. An order of an appellate court used when the court exercises discretion about whether or not to hear an appeal. If the writ is denied, the court refuses to hear the appeal and the decision of the court that previously heard the case remains in effect. If the writ is granted, the appellate court will reconsider the case and perhaps change the decision of the lower court.

Writ of error. A writ issued from an appeals court to a trial court requiring the trial court to send the record of a case to the appeals court for reconsideration. The writ is based on errors of law apparent from the record. It is the beginning of a new suit to reverse a decision of a lower court and is not a continuation of any suit in a lower court.

Writ of habeus corpus. Literally, "you have the body." The primary function of this writ is to force the release of a person from unlawful imprisonment.